PARISH:

A PLACE FOR WORSHIP

Edited by
Mark Searle

THE LITURGICAL PRESS—Collegeville, Minnesota

Papers from the Ninth Annual Conference of the Notre Dame Center for Pastoral Liturgy, University of Notre Dame, June 16–19, 1980.

Nihil obstat: Robert C. Harren, *Censor deputatus.*
Imprimatur: ✠ George H. Speltz, D.D., Bishop of St. Cloud. August 3, 1981.
Copyright © 1981 by The Order of St. Benedict, Inc., Collegeville, Minnesota. All rights reserved. No part of this book may be reproduced or transmitted in any form or by any means, electronic or mechanical, including photocopying, recording, taping, or any information storage and retrieval system, without the written permission of The Liturgical Press, Collegeville, Minnesota 56321.
Printed in the United States of America.
Cover design by Fred Petters.

Library of Congress Cataloging in Publication Data
Main entry under title:

Parish, a place for worship.

    1. Catholic Church—Liturgy—Congresses. 2. Parishes—Congresses. I. Searle, Mark, 1941– . II. Notre Dame Center for Pastoral Liturgy.
BX1970.A1P35   264'.02   81–13655
ISBN 0-8146-1236-9 (pbk.)   AACR2

Contents

Introduction 5
Mark Searle

I. PERSPECTIVES ON PARISH WORSHIP

The Parish We Are Shaping 13
Richard P. McBrien
The Parish That Shaped Us 29
Philip Murnion
The Parish in the American Past 51
Jay Dolan and Jeffrey Burns

II. ISSUES IN PARISH WORSHIP

The Sense of the Sacred 65
Nathan Mitchell, O.S.B.
Liturgical Creativity 81
Louis Weil
New Forms of Parish Ministry 97
Regis Duffy, O.F.M.

III. CASES OF PARISH LIFE AND WORSHIP

The Urban Church 121
Edward M. Miller
The Rural Parish 137
Mary Ann Simcoe
The Alternative Parish 155
Dolly Sokol and Jack Doherty

1980 MICHAEL MATHIS AWARD TO MSGR. MARTIN HELLRIEGEL

Liturgical Pioneers and Parish Worship 181
Frederick R. McManus

To Martin Hellriegel
1890–1981

Introduction

MARK SEARLE

Like any other human community, the parish is a complex, multi-faceted phenomenon. Like any other community, it has its structures, both formal and informal, and a seemingly endless list of functions which occupy its members in their role as parishioners or members of the parish staff. The celebration of the liturgy often seems to be one more kind of activity, welcome or onerous depending on one's point of view. Not infrequently, the celebration of the liturgy appears, especially to the parish professionals, as a fairly routine, necessary, but not particularly efficient pastoral task. Acknowledgement is given to the "grace of the sacraments" and the "value of the Mass," but when judged in terms of the expenditure of time, energy, and financial resources, liturgy actually occupies a lowly place on the list of priorities—unless maintenance of the ecclesiastical plant be entered under the cult column.

This is lamentable for two reasons. First, it fails to recognize that for the majority of Catholics their sole point of contact with the Church is in the liturgical assembly. In other words, whatever other priorities the clergy and staff may have in their pastoral ministry, the majority of their parishioners consider the parish to be preeminently a place for worship. It is the impression of the local community as this is encountered at Sunday Mass and in the celebration of the occasional sacraments which shapes their feelings and expectations about the religious community at large. For many, too, Sunday worship is, far more than adult education courses or seasonal programs, a significant factor in the making or breaking of their faith life. The number of people who actually come to the rectory for counselling or to the school for continuing education is miniscule in comparison with the number who turn up for Mass. In this, the practice of parish staffs often fails to match the expectations of parish people that the parish be, above all else, a place for worship. The fruits are to be seen across the land in liturgical celebrations that are listless in tone, didactic in character.

Second, the failure of most parishes to make the community prayer of the liturgy a priority results in the widespread failure of parish liturgy to provide a focal point and integrating factor for the rest of the parish activities. Too often, parishes lack any clear sense of direction and purpose; the liturgy, which could provide both vision and inspiration, then becomes itself rote and uninspiring. Moreover, what happens at the level of parish life is reflected in the personal lives of the faithful. If parish liturgy is just one more parish activity, going to Mass remains at the level of one of the things Catholics have to do; but if the liturgy of a parish in fact finds its roots in the wider life of the community, then the people themselves will be brought to overcome what Vatican II denounced as the disastrous split between the faith we profess and our experience of life in the world.

For these reasons, and acting out of a conviction about the centrality of Christian worship in the common life of Christian people, the Notre Dame Center for Pastoral Liturgy decided to dedicate its 1980 June Conference to the theme *Parish: A Place for Worship*. This choice of theme was in no way intended to suggest that the parish is the only place for worship; nor that the parish has no other function than to provide opportunities for worship; but only to promote the view that, whatever else a parish is about, it is about the common prayer and celebration of the People of God.

The annual June Conference both symbolizes the Center's desire to serve as a meeting-place for people in different fields and is an effective means to the realization of that desire. For that reason, as well as in the hope of doing justice to the complexities of parish worship, the speakers were chosen for their different backgrounds and for their excellence in their different areas of the apostolate. The contributors to this book represent specializations in American Church history, ecclesiology, sociology of religion, liturgical history, and liturgical theology; as well as pastoral practitioners in widely differing contexts, from the ghettoes of the Northeast to the cornfields of the Midwest.

While a more rigorous study of the subject yet remains to be done, it was our concern to suggest in broad brush strokes both the problems and the possibilities of parish worship in the United States today. For this reason, too, the papers presented here are more representative of the present situation of the American Church than advocating the realization of specific future goals. It was our conviction that priests and people at parish level are more in need of help in taking stock of where they are today than of grandiose visions of a new Church for tomorrow. These papers represent a survey of what we have inherited, where we now stand, what problems cry out to be tackled, and what opportunities present themselves as indicating the way to go from here.

There are, of course, individual contributors who dwell more than others on the future, but it is the overall impact of this collection that matters. Of course, some of what is said will appear radically innovative, even futuristic, in some parishes and will be taken as reflecting current thinking and practice in others. Such are the risks of trying to address the mainstream of American Catholicism and to reflect the variety of experiences of being a Catholic community which are available in this country today. Nevertheless, for all the differences of approach and emphasis, a number of themes emerge as matters of consensus and as indicating the direction in which parish worship might develop.

First (and here it is worth remembering the diversity of our contributors), the hierarchical and institutional model of Church and parish seems to be in deep trouble. Again and again the writers testify to the emergence of new ways of being Church, ways which allow of considerable variation in structural details but are characterized by the abandonment of the inherited dichotomy between clerical ministry and lay passivity. The recognition of different models of Church has moved out of the pages of theological writing and become a fact of life among the parishes of this country. There is every indication that this development is going to continue, thereby introducing a much greater variety of parishes into a Church which, in recent times at least, has been characterized — or has liked to think of itself as characterized — by monolithic uniformity, to the point where pastors could be moved around *ad nutum episcopi* without reference to them or to their people, and where the same principle operated at the diocesan level in the appointment and translation of bishops. Consultation at all levels is still in its initial stages, but it is perhaps a harbinger of things to come and a form of remote preparation for decisions which are going to have to be made in the not too distant future about parish leadership as a result of the seemingly irreversible decline of the present clerical system. The connections between this reordering of relationships within the community of the Church and the celebration of the liturgy at parish level are manifold, as the papers in this collection reveal.

This leads to a second and related theme recurring in these pages, namely, that the cultivation of the laity's active participation in the liturgy requires, if it is to be done with integrity, their participation in all areas of parish life. In other words, the recognition that the gathered community is the true subject of liturgical celebration necessarily implies that the local Christian community, if it is to be an ecclesial community at all, must be allowed to be the dirigent of its own life. A clientele is not a community: a community is a moral person, a subject of corresponding rights and responsibilities. We have taken the first step in recognizing, to some degree at least, that this is true in worship: the celebrant of the liturgy is the congregation itself. But this step forward will remain halfhearted and hesitant wherever the full implications of congregational participation are not recognized and embraced by clergy and laity alike.

Third, it also becomes clear that there is a consensus among our contributors concerning the extent and direction of such newly acknowledged rights and responsibilities. If the new spirit abroad in the Church means no more than "power-sharing," nothing significant will have been achieved. On the other hand, the new sense of collective identity and mutual accountability should lead, and in places is already leading, to a sense of the accountability of the parish before God for the wider community in whose midst it lives. By breaking out of the individualistic spirituality which has formed us, we are on our way to recovering a sense of our common vocation to be at the service of all God's children. This, in turn, engenders a new sense of mission — in the sense both of service and of evangelization — and a corresponding awareness of the social dimensions of sin and of grace.

Fourth, these papers suggest that the recovery of this relationship with the larger, secular world will in turn be echoed in the liturgical celebrations of the believers. The expectation, based on the experiences of communities who have already reached this point, is that worship will be less tightly scheduled, more relaxed in its pace, more related to the social and geographical location of the community concerned, more reflective of the joys, hopes, aspirations, struggles, and fears of the people who gather for prayer. There is likely to be greater diversity from one parish to another, less uniformity of style, less centralization in decision-making, more utilization of the resources and talents of the local people.

What we see in this collection of papers is parish life and worship not so much breaking with the past as struggling imaginatively with the challenges of the present and future. Over the whole enterprise there is cast the shadow of a question which is nowhere made explicit: how is the Church to adapt to the new situation brought about by the diminishing number and advancing age of the clergy? The question is not raised explicitly because this is not the place for speculative answers. Instead, we have the picture of an American Church taking stock of its parochial life and worship and discovering within itself and within its tradition the resources to meet the challenges of what may be a very different tomorrow. Only one thing is certain in this uncertain future: the parish will remain a place for worship.

Finally, there is one more theme running through this book, less obvious perhaps than the others, but no less important: the theme of being responsible for handing on a living tradition. Taking our bearings for the future, we find ourselves remembering our past — our American past, our Christian past — and with that, the memory of those who have gone before us marked with the sign of faith. This acknowledgement of the past permits it both to judge us and to inspire us, while making us grateful for the gifts we have received and for those who, under God, have been bearers of the tradition in their time. The Michael Mathis Award, named after the great liturgical pioneer from Notre Dame, permits us to recognize those whose lives and ministries have contributed significantly to the renewal of the Church's worship life. On the occasion of this Conference devoted to parish liturgy, it was altogether fitting that the award should have been presented to one of America's outstanding pastors, Msgr. Martin Hellriegel of the archdiocese of St. Louis. His contribution, together with that of his fellow pioneers, is recognized and appraised by Msgr. Frederick McManus in a postscript to this volume, "Liturgical Pioneers and Parish Worship." Monsignor Hellriegel, prevented by sickness and age from attending the Conference, died at age ninety on April 10, 1981. We commend him to the Master he had served so long and so well, and we dedicate this volume respectfully and gratefully to his memory.

I. PERSPECTIVES ON PARISH WORSHIP

The Parish We Are Shaping

RICHARD MCBRIEN

In this presentation on the meaning of parish, I shall propose three theological principles. First, a parish is a local church, that is, the Body of Christ present in a particular place. Second, because it is a local church, the parish has the same mission and the same basic structure as the Church universal. Third, because the parish participates in the nature and mission of the Church universal, our model of the latter will shape our understanding of the nature and mission of the parish. Or, to put the third principle in different words, our theology of parish is inevitably a reflection of our theology of the Church itself — our ecclesiology.

Following a description and explanation of these three theological principles, I shall suggest how these principles relate to questions of ministry, catholicity, and liturgy. These suggestions will, in turn, prepare the way for reflection in our parishes by raising such questions as: What should the future parish be doing by way of Christian service? How should it relate itself to other communities, both inside and outside the Body of Christ? And how should its worship reflect both its service to, and its bonds of communion with, others?

RICHARD MCBRIEN is Crowley-O'Brien-Walter Professor of Theology at the University of Notre Dame and chairman of the theology department. He is past president of the Catholic Theological Society of America and author of twelve books, including the recent two-volume work *Catholicism*. He is a priest of the archdiocese of Hartford.

I. Parish as Local Church

What does it mean, first of all, to say that the parish is a local church? The term "local church" has both canonical and theological significance. Canonically, the term "local church" is closely related to the term "particular church" which, in turn, refers to a diocese. Both terms—"local church" and "particular church"—are used in the documents of Vatican II, the latter more frequently than the former. On at least one occasion, however, the terms are used interchangeably: "This most sacred Synod gladly reminds all of one highly significant fact among others: in the East there flourish many particular or local Churches. . . ."[1]

Theology is less constricted in its understanding of "local church" than is canon law. In ecclesiology the term "local church" applies to any integral manifestation of the Body of Christ in a particular place. By "integral manifestation" I mean a more or less stable group of Christians, i.e., those who confess and practice the Lordship of Jesus, who gather on a regular basis for the celebration of the Eucharist, who have a sense of common mission, and whose community is shaped and guided in some measure by various ministries. There are, of course, degrees of "integral manifestation" or of "locality." Accordingly, a "local church" may be a diocese, a national church, a so-called specialized community, or indeed what we have traditionally known as a parish. In this context, a parish is a local church which is, in turn, part of a larger community of local churches known as the diocese.

Catholics, not surprisingly, have differed on their understanding of the nature and future of the parish. From the left, there are those who insist that the day of the parish is over. Organizing the Christian community according to neighborhood or residential lines is obsolete and pastorally counterpro-

---

1. Decree on Ecumenism, *The Documents of Vatican II*, ed. Walter Abbot (New York: Association Press, 1966) 14. All quotations from Vatican II documents in this paper are from this edition.

ductive, it is argued. And, from the right, there are those who look upon the parish not as a local church, but simply as an administrative subdivision of the Church universal.

Let us take the left-of-center critique of the parish first. It may be so, of course, that the parish is an outmoded form of Christian existence, but convincing evidence has not yet been brought forth to satisfy most people. In any case, this left-of-center challenge to the existence of the parish is a healthy reminder that our first theological principle has an important corollary, namely, that while the parish is a local church, not all local churches are parishes. Or, to put the matter differently, there are several ways of realizing the Body of Christ, of bringing specific Christian communities into being. Gathering the assembly according to geographical proximity is only one, although clearly it is the most common, the most convenient, and perhaps, therefore, the most pastorally desirable.

But the mere assembling of a group of Christians in a particular place for some common purpose does not necessarily make the group a church. It is not enough that people regularly come together to call them a church. When *does* a group of Christians in a particular place become a church?

Before Vatican II that question may not have made any sense to a Catholic. People do not *become* the Church; they *join* it. In recent years, however, the question has assumed increasing importance. More and more often, religiously motivated people have gathered together in small groups for common prayer, mutual support, and perhaps even joint action on behalf of the needy or in some public cause.

In some cases, the members of such groups regard themselves as outsiders to official, institutional Christianity. They may no longer attend their own churches nor retain any allegiance toward their denominational bureaucracies. And yet they have a sense of community, sometimes a very profound experience of it. They see themselves as a kind of church within the Church or even as a church *against* the Church. Although they continue to employ much of the traditional language of Christianity and many of its customs, these groups at times include within their ranks men and women whom the official churches would not recognize as Christians.

Catholics should not be completely surprised by this development. In a sense, it has reflected the renewed emphasis of the Second Vatican Council on the local church. "This Church of Christ is truly present in all legitimate local congregations of the faithful," the Council declared in its Dogmatic Constitution on the Church. "For in their own locality these are the new people called by God, in the Holy Spirit. . . ."[2]

The question is: How do we determine legitimacy? Unless we want to deny to the word "church" all its theological, sociological, and historical meaning, it cannot be used so indiscriminately that it applies to whatever we want it to. It is an entirely contemporary phenomenon that people (usually left-of-center Christians disenchanted with the quality of official leadership) are ready to apply the term "church" to groups which might just as likely include some who are not Christians and which welcome these non-Christians to full participation in whatever liturgy they have.

It seems, however, that the same Council which promoted and celebrated the reality of the local church within the Church universal also provided, here and there, some criteria by which such local assemblages might in fact be identified as ecclesial in nature.

1. They must confess Jesus of Nazareth as the Christ and Lord of history.[3]
2. They must be summoned together by the proclamation of, and in response to, the word of God embodied in Sacred Scripture.[4]

---

2. Constitution on the Church 26.
3. Pastoral Constitution on the Church in the Modern World 10.
4. Constitution on the Church 25–26.

3. They must be moved to express their response sacramentally, especially in baptism and the Eucharist.[5]

4. They must have a sense of common purpose and common responsibility for the application of the gospel of Jesus Christ to the situation around them.[6]

5. They must designate some of their membership to fulfill specific services (ministries) for the sake of such a mission; these ministries are, in a Catholic local church, united by the pastoral ministry of the bishops and of the chief bishop.[7]

There are, of course, degrees of ecclesial reality. A community without the fifth quality — having to do with ministry — is, to some real extent, deficient, but it may still be called a "church." On the other hand, a community without the first quality — belief in the Lordship of Jesus — cannot be called a church in any sense, at least not without rewriting the history of the last twenty centuries. Our newer experiences and insights may encourage us to apply the word "church" more broadly than before. But they do not allow us to drain the word of all meaning so that it applies wherever we find friendship and sharing of any kind. Not every community is a church. Not every community of *Christians* is a church, even if all of them are members of the Church.

And what of the second misconception of the meaning of the parish, namely, the right-of-center assumption that the parish is only an administrative subdivision of the Church universal? This second view represents a similarly serious misunderstanding of the nature of the Church.

The assertion that a parish is simply an administrative subdivision of the Church universal is predicated on the assumption that the Church is a monarchical institution, with the pope as its absolute ruler. The Church is, as it were, one large diocese, with the pope as its single shepherd. The diocese is, in turn, divided

5. Decree on Ecumenism 22.
6. *Ibid.* 23.
7. Constitution on the Church 18.

into smaller units, each governed by the pope's vicar, the bishop. If the bishop were able to take care of the needs of his whole territory alone, he would. But because this would be impossible, the bishop, in turn, subdivides his territory and places *his own* vicars over these subunits. These representatives of the bishop are called pastors.

According to this view, there is no question of the Body of Christ being fully present in a diocesan subunit, known to us as the parish. The parish exists only for the purpose of administrative convenience. The parish can do nothing, and indeed is nothing, without the direct approval and support of the pope, who, according to canon law, has immediate and universal jurisdiction over the entire Church.

This notion of the parish as simply an administrative subunit of the Church universal ignores or misunderstands the meaning of collegiality (and is also inconsistent with the history of the Church—a point to which I shall return later). Collegiality means more than coresponsibility between pope and bishops. Collegiality, in its deepest sense, means that the Church universal is itself a communion of local churches, that the Body of Christ is composed of a vast international network of local churches which themselves represent and manifest the Body of Christ in a particular place.

Indeed, the recovery of the theology of the local church at the Second Vatican Council was a necessary and almost inevitable outcome of the recovery of the doctrine of collegiality. Nowhere is the Council's teaching on the importance of the local church more clearly expressed than in the Dogmatic Constitution on the Church (no. 26, to which I referred earlier):

> This Church of Christ is truly present in all legitimate local congregations of the faithful which, united with their pastors, are themselves called churches in the New Testament. For in their own locality these are the new people called by God, in the Holy Spirit and in much fullness. In them the faithful are gathered together by the preaching of the gospel of Christ, and the mystery of the Lord's Supper is celebrated. . . .

> In these communities, . . . Christ is present. By virtue of Him the one, holy, catholic, and apostolic Church gathers together. For "the partaking of the Body and Blood of Christ does nothing other than transform us into that which we consume."

Throughout the history of the Church, however, there has been a tension between those who have emphasized the universality of Christ's Body and those who have emphasized its particularity in a specific place. Roman Catholicism through most of the twentieth century has stressed universality (and with it a highly centralized style of governance), while the Baptist tradition, for example, has stressed particularity, the sovereignty of the parish. At the Second Vatican Council, the Catholic Church began moving back closer to the center, toward recovering the importance of the local church without denying the basic collegial principle that the Body of Christ is itself a communion of local churches and that a given local church is not really within that Body unless it is at the same time in communion with the other churches.

This highly institutionalized, almost bureaucratic, understanding of parish is also contradicted by the New Testament and by the early history of the Church. There is no single New Testament ecclesiology. The Church of the New Testament is at once local and universal, but not in the sense that the local church is simply a subdivision of the Church universal, nor that the Church universal is simply the sum total of local churches. In the earliest layers of New Testament ecclesiology, the Church happens always in a particular place: Jerusalem first, then also Corinth, Antioch, and so forth. Only much later, in the letters to the Ephesians and the Colossians, do we even begin to detect an understanding of the Body of Christ as universal.

Although the relationship between the universal and local expressions of the Body of Christ is not made precise in the New Testament, it is clear that we do not have a Corinthian division of the Church, for example, but "the church of God which is in Corinth" (1 Cor 1:2; see also 2 Cor 1:1). On the other hand, the

Church universal is a living, integrated organism: "the fullness of him who fills the universe in all its parts" (Eph 1:23).

The diversity from one local church to another is also remarkable. The original Jerusalem community, for example, maintained its close links with Judaism: there is a strong attachment to the Temple (Acts 6:13-14; 7), the continuation of Jewish practices, and the voluntary community of goods. There is also within this original Jerusalem community evidence of conflict: for example, between Jewish and Greek members over the care of widows (Acts 6:1-6) and, of course, the great debate over the need for circumcision and the observance of Jewish dietary laws (Acts 15:1-31).

On the other hand, the church at Antioch, the third largest city in the Roman Empire, was a model of harmony between Jews and Gentiles (Gal 2:1-14). Prophets and teachers were active here (Acts 13:1-3), and the gifts of the Spirit were evident (Acts 11:27; 15:32).

The church of Corinth, finally, was marked by a strongly charismatic character (1 Cor 1:5-7; 12:8-11) and by certain human weaknesses to match. The charismatics, we are told, often created confusion (1 Cor 14). Serious disorders arose at the celebration of the Eucharist because of the behavior of the rich (1 Cor 11:20-34). Partisan groups attached to particular missionaries emerged (1 Cor 1:11). Many sided against Paul, as his second letter to the Corinthians suggests. Pagan vices prevailed (1 Cor 5; 6:12-30). And yet the church at Corinth flourished: there was a rich apostolic preaching and instruction (2 Cor 3:4 – 4:6). Worship occupied a central place (1 Cor 11:17-34). Baptism and Eucharist were sources of deep religious experience (1 Cor 1:13-16; 6:11; 10:1-11, 16-22). It was a church in fellowship with the church of Jerusalem, for which the great collection was taken up, and in fellowship with other churches (1 Cor 1:2; 7:17; 11:16; 16:1, 19; 2 Cor 1:1; 8:24; 12:13; 13:12).

Despite all local differences among the Jewish-Christian, the Jewish-Hellenistic, and the Hellenistic-Gentile communities of the New Testament, common elements stood out clearly then as they do now among all local churches which together constitute the Body of Christ: faith in Jesus as Messiah and Lord, the practice of baptism and the celebration of the Eucharist, the apostolic preaching and instruction, the high regard for communal love, and the expectation of the coming kingdom of God. Great freedom was allowed in other matters—as it is not always allowed today—a freedom which, when exercised, manifested the limitations as well as the spiritual grandeur of the whole Church.

II. THE MISSION OF THE PARISH

My second theological principle: Because it is a local church, that is, the Body of Christ in a particular place, the parish has the same mission and the same basic structure as the Church universal.

The place and function of the Church universal and in each of its local manifestations must be seen against the horizon of the coming kingdom of God. This was the horizon for Jesus' preaching and ministry, his death and resurrection, and so it is the horizon for the Church's participation in that mission.

The Church exists, first of all, to proclaim that the kingdom of God has found its definitive expression in Jesus of Nazareth and that it will be brought to final perfection in him and through the power of the Holy Spirit. Humankind has been radically liberated from sin and death, from fear and selfishness. The message of the gospel is, as Pope John Paul II put it in *Redemptor hominis*, that we are worth something—every individual woman, man, and child. No one is expendable.[8]

But the Church must be prepared to discern and to expose the gaps which inevitably continue to exist between the institutions and structures of our society, on the one hand, and the promised kingdom of God which is to be given at the end of history, on the other. When the Church calls attention to this

---

8. Encyclical Letter *Redemptor hominis* 13 and *passim*.

gap between the kingdom-of-promise and the world as it is, the Church is engaged in the ministry of prophetic judgment. And this, too, is part of its kerygmatic task.

Because the Church really believes that Jesus of Nazareth is the Lord, that his gospel is the ground, the goal, and the hope of all human history, it joyfully and thankfully celebrates this faith, especially in its great act of thanksgiving, the Eucharist. It remembers the definitive inbreaking of the kingdom in Jesus Christ, it points to its present inbreaking disclosed in the signs of the times and in our ordinary everyday experiences, and it looks toward its final coming at the end of history.

If the local church or parish is to be faithful to its mission, therefore, it must be a community which acknowledges in word and in sacrament the Lordship of Jesus and the coming kingdom of God and which prophetically denounces whatever seems to contradict or suppress the gospel of Jesus Christ and the coming kingdom of God.

The Church exists, furthermore, as the embodiment of the kingdom which it proclaims and celebrates. The Church must offer itself as a test case of its own preaching. It must be able to say to the world, "See! This is what happens when men and women are open to the word of God and allow themselves to be transformed by the Lord's and the Spirit's presence!"

The Church must be that kind of community which gives people hope in the final outcome of history, "By thus giving witness to the truth, . . . men and women throughout the world will be aroused to a lively hope — the gift of the Holy Spirit — that they will finally be caught up in peace and utter happiness in that kingdom radiant with the splendor of the Lord."[9] The Church must be a fellowship of such quality, therefore, that people find themselves being ennobled and enriched by participation in its life. The Church is not simply an agent of social change moving here and there, wherever the action happens to

---

9. Pastoral Constitution 9.

be. It is a community. As such, it must be a credible sign (by its life of faith, hope, charity, and the free pursuit of truth) — a sign of the presence of the triumphant grace of Christ in history. If the local church or parish is to be faithful to its mission, therefore, it must be a community of such a kind that it inspires respect and emulation rather than cynical rejection or indifference.

The Church exists, finally, to be the facilitator, enabler, or instrument of the kingdom of God. The Church does not create, build, or establish the kingdom. That is the work of God alone. However, the Church does have some special collaborative role in the kingdom's realization. There is some real continuity, in other words, between what we do here within human history and what God will bestow upon us at the end of history: "Earthly progress must be carefully distinguished from the growth of Christ's kingdom. Nevertheless, to the extent that the former can contribute to the latter ordering of human society, it is of vital concern to the kingdom of God."[10]

Wherever genuine community happens, it happens because of the Spirit's presence. The Church's function is to facilitate the transforming presence of God, to enable it to work unto the creation of community, to be a willing instrument of forgiveness, reconciliation, justice, peace, compassion, and so forth. This responsibility brings the Church into the social and political spheres, because this is where such issues are joined. The Church's *diakonia* is not competitive with the political agencies; it is prophetic and supplementary, that is, the Church reminds society of its neglected human priorities, and it offers its own resources to assist society in confronting and resolving these human problems. It is a matter, therefore, of reading "the signs of the times" and responding to them creatively and effectively.[11]

If the local church or parish is to be faithful to its mission, therefore, it must also be a community which is open to the

10. *Ibid.* 39.
11. *Ibid.* 4–10.

challenges of socio-political involvement and which willingly but intelligently allocates its resources for the sake of realizing God's reign among us—a reign of charity, justice, truth, freedom, and peace.

In measuring the effectiveness of a parish, therefore, we must bring these theological standards to bear upon its stated commitments and performance. The Church exists for the kingdom of God—to proclaim it in word and sacrament, to be a credible sign of it through its community life, and to be its agent through generous service to the cause of justice, peace, and human rights. And so, too, does the parish exist for the sake of the kingdom of God.

III. Parish and Models of Church

My third theological principle: Because the parish participates in the nature and mission of the Church universal, our model of the Church universal will shape our understanding of the nature and mission of the parish.

Limitations of space do not permit even a full outline of ecclesiological models here. Extensive treatment appears in chapter 20 of my work *Catholicism* and in Avery Dulles' *Models of the Church*.[12] It is enough to say here that I prefer three basic models to Avery Dulles' five: [1] the Church as institution, [2] the Church as community, and [3] the Church as agent of social change, or servant. Each of these models says something true about the Church, but no model by itself captures the full scope of the Church's nature and mission.

To understand the Church primarily as an institution is to see it as a visible society, hierarchically structured, which exists to mediate salvation through word and sacrament. The

---

12. Richard McBrien, *Catholicism* (Minneapolis: Winston Press, 1980); Avery Dulles, *Models of the Church* (Garden City, N.Y.: Doubleday & Co., 1974).

strengths of this model are several: its sense of tradition, its respect for history and continuity, its sense of order, its strong sense of identity. But the weaknesses of the institutional model are also many: its clericalism, its legalism, its triumphalism, its impersonalism. Those who follow the institutional model of Church are more likely to see the parish primarily as an administrative unit of the diocese and a subunit of the Church universal. As such, the parish has no pastoral sovereignty of its own; everything it does that even begins to be important, it does with clearance from the bishop or the chancery. In its governance, the parish is under the unilateral leadership of the pastor, who is, in turn, responsible directly to the bishop. If there is a parish council, it can never be more than an advisory body. The same ecclesiological perspective is evident in the recent liturgical document from the Sacred Congregation for the Sacraments and Divine Worship.[13]

Second, to understand the Church primarily as a community or a people brings us closer not only to the Second Vatican Council but also to the New Testament. The community model is freed of most of the drawbacks of the institutional model of Church. But the community model has its own characteristic weaknesses. There can be so much emphasis on spontaneity and freedom that lines of responsibility become blurred and so much stress on personal authenticity and commitment that a responsibility for the tradition is diminished. Those who understand the Church according to a community model are more likely to see the parish as encompassing the whole congregation, laity as well as clergy and religious, and to see the decision-making process as a common responsibility of the whole community. The community principle can distort our understanding of parish only when it brings us to the point of equating the

---

13. Instruction on Eucharistic Worship, issued by the Congregation for the Sacraments and Divine Worship, dated April 3, 1980, issued May 23, 1980. English text in *Origins* 10, no. 3 (June 5, 1980) 41-44.

reality of community with the reality of Church, so that where there is community (even if the Lordship of Jesus is not accepted by all), there is the Church. And if there is the Church, there is a common basis for the celebration of the Eucharist. Correspondingly, the community principle can be carried too far when ordination or communion with the bishop and the pope are no longer regarded as of any significant account. On the other hand, the true values of the community model are suppressed — as in the Instruction on Eucharistic Worship — when liturgy is celebrated in such a way that only the role of the presiding priest is italicized, and abuses are always and only those of a laity encroaching upon the territory of the clergy.

Third, to understand the Church primarily as an agent of social change or a servant is to see it as a prophetic movement, committed to the kingdom of justice and peace. The servant model saves the Church from an introverted existence and indeed from failing to fulfill an essential part of its mission. The servant model emphasizes the social and political implications of Christian existence more explicitly than the community model — and certainly more than the institution model. But there is an equivalent risk in the servant model, especially when pursued too single-mindedly, of eventually suppressing or minimizing the abiding mission of preaching and sacramental celebration, or even of "manipulating" the liturgical texts "for social and political ends," as the recent liturgical document warned. On occasion, in the interest of social justice, we can forget that the Church is also, at the same time, called to be a sacrament of Christ's presence. A form of action, even for the sake of justice, which tears the Church apart is a form of action which can render ineffective the Church's sacramental mission. This is not to countenance a missionary timidity or conservatism in the face of injustice and oppression of various kinds, but only to suggest that there are criteria by which to determine when, how, and under what circumstances the Church should apply its limited resources in the public forum.

IV. Conclusions

By way of conclusion, I offer here some pastoral implications flowing from these three ecclesiological principles.

1. Regarding *ministry*. We must continue to emphasize the baptismal responsibility of everyone to witness to the gospel and to participate fully in the life of the Church according to its needs and their own ability and opportunities. In that sense, ministry is an empowerment to serve others and, as such, is universal in scope. But we cannot forget at the same time that there is also a specific and formal character to ministry. It is a service to which the Church calls certain qualified persons to assist in the fulfillment of its mission. Since these formal ministries are exercised in the service of the Church and in its name, the Church has both the right and the responsibility to pass judgment on the admission, supervision, and evaluation of candidates for ministry. As a bare minimum, all such candidates must be humanly and religiously whole and must have a fundamentally sound vision of the nature and mission of the Church they presume to serve and in whose name they propose to act. We must also be prepared to create new ministries and to abolish old ones.

2. Regarding *catholicity, or communion*. The Church lives always in creative tension. One of these is the tension between universality and particularity. The Church is at once the Church universal and the local church; indeed, the former is a communion of local churches (collegiality). To be Catholic means, among other things, to be an integral part of the family of Catholic communities and to shape one's corporate life with the values of sacramentality, mediation, and peoplehood, or communion.[14] But we cannot confuse creative tension with mutual opposition. The Church universal is not necessarily the enemy of the local church, as in the case of the recent liturgical directive from the Vatican. It is a matter of balancing, of fine tuning, of

---

14. McBrien, *Catholicism* 2:1169–86.

dialectical relationship, of both/and rather than of either/or. Organization is for mission, not vice versa. The Church can be overorganized or underorganized.

3. Regarding *liturgy*. The Church is still in the very early stages of its history (What is A.D. 1980 in light of A.D. 201, 980?). If this is a time of crisis, it is also a time of opportunity (*krinein* = to choose).[15] Our choices, however, can never be arbitrary, but neither can they be constrained by a confusion of essence and accidents, substance and forms. If liturgy is, as Karl Rahner once wrote, the highest, most visible moment when the Church becomes "event," and if the Church is, in turn, a genuinely world-Church and not only the Church of Europe and North America, then its liturgies will be as richly diverse as the cultural spectrum of its membership.

But we have to attend all the while to the questions of substance and of continuity. History *relativizes*, that is, forms need not be as they are. But history also *roots*, that is, our very identity as Christians and as Catholics is to be found there. We cannot create that identity anew each day any more than we can repeal our family histories and begin again when and where we wish. It is part of the facticity of our existence, and it is also that facticity that we bring to the table of the Eucharist: our sex, our race, our national character, our physical resources, our gifts, and so on.

When all is said and done, we must proceed on the basis of a vision of who we are and what we are about: ecclesiology and escatology, for starters, but also anthropology, a theology of God, and christology. This demands knowledge, insight, understanding, judgment, and the readiness to act on it. It is clear beyond any reasonable doubt that the liturgist, the religious educator, and the theologian are natural and necessary collaborators in this ongoing task. May our collaboration continue to be at once constructive and fruitful.

---

15. *Ibid.* 3–15, 605–56.

The Parish That Shaped Us

PHILIP J. MURNION

Each person is a continually developing mosaic. The myriad, variegated fragments of our being are the contributions of all the persons and events in our lives. Some impressions are the result of deliberate attempts to color our approaches to life. Some are the surprising consequences of chance occurrences. There is no accounting for all of these impressions on us, but to the extent that we are aware of what is happening to us or even begin to reflect on the many parts of who we are, we play a decisive role in the ultimate composition of ourselves. We can never remove any of these markings on our being, but we can decide their relative intensity and the shape of the final image.

The continuing mission of Christ is to bring us to the radical freedom necessary for us to become cocreators of our own lives. Christ brings us the freedom and power to become the person God intended each of us to be and provides us with the basic model of personhood for our creative efforts. But Christ does not extract us from the world or lift us out of the flesh of our experience. In fact, when praying for his followers at the Last Supper, he explicitly says to the Father that he is not asking him to remove them from the world but to aid them in the world. Fur-

---

PHILIP MURNION is director of the parish project of the National Conference of Catholic Bishops. A priest of the archdiocese of New York, he holds a doctorate in sociology.

thermore, even the action of Christ comes to us largely through the persons and events of our lives.

The first and most important influences on our lives come from our *families*. No influence on our sense of ourselves, our relationships with others, our images of God, our understanding of life, or our relationship with the Church compares with the influence exerted by our families. Family influence has always been evident, and recent studies of what helps people to remain strong in faith and in commitment to the Church only serve to confirm this influence. In affecting our religious lives, the families that formed us are surpassed only by the families we form.

A second source of influence on our religious lives is the *culture* within which we live and grow. The values, the meanings we assign to aspects of our lives, and the ways we express ourselves are all deeply influenced by the cultural patterns of our own people. Whether we view God as primarily loving or demanding, merciful or just, compassionate or judgmental is often conditioned by the views communicated to us in numerous ways by our people. Whether the Church is important or relatively insignificant will be determined largely by the history of the Church's place in our people's lives and in our culture. Whether we are basically optimistic or pessimistic about life varies among ethnic groups.

A third influence on our religious lives is the *Church*, though it is already clear that its influence varies in style and intensity from person to person. For most people, the Church is largely the parish, although in recent years increased public reporting on the larger Church has made the universal Church more immediate to people. The influence of the parish itself has been very strong among some people and marginal for others. Chicago historian Ellen Skerret reports that the parish was more important to Chicago's Polish immigrants than to its Irish immigrants, partially because Polish-speaking Catholics had greater difficulty participating in other organizations than did the English-speaking Irish.[1]

The history of Mexican-American Catholics indicates that the absence of native clergy sympathetic with their piety made them much more dependent for their religious lives on their family religious practices than on the parish, as has been true also for most Puerto Ricans.

I have tried to put the topic of this paper—the parish that shaped us—in context by insisting on some modesty about the shaping influence of the parish in relation to other forces. The parish was *one of many* shaping forces. Nonetheless, the parish did mediate the Church to most people and, especially where the family actively supported the influence of the parish, this influence was often quite profound.

With this background, I will approach the question of the influence of the parish in five steps: first, by exploring how both intentional and unintentional influence occurs; second, by sketching some of the dominant influences of the past; third, by suggesting some of the intentional influences of the parish in present patterns of renewal; fourth, by pointing to some unintended influences in parish ministry today; and fifth, by suggesting some concerns as to whether the shape of Christian life promoted by the parish today will meet the challenges of religious life in our time.

I. Formation Intended and Unintended

A good example of the complicated process by which basic approaches to religious life develop can be found in that classic work of liturgical scholarship by Dom Gregory Dix, *The Shape of the Liturgy*. Dix describes the process through which the cele-

---

1. Ellen Skerret, "The Irish and Polish Parish: Chicago 1880-1920" (Paper delivered at the American Catholic Studies Seminar, University of Notre Dame, March 7, 1981).

bration of the Mass became an occasion for private, devotional meditation on the Passion and death of Jesus. In the fourth century, the Church suddenly found itself with massive numbers of new members, the barbarians. Because of the brutal lives of these people, great emphasis was placed on moral teaching rather than doctrine. Moreover, the Church began to underscore St. Paul's warning against approaching the Eucharist unworthily and discouraged people from receiving the Eucharist frequently.

Gradually, Communion came to be regarded as the regular prerogative of only the priest, and with this came reduction of people's participation, first in the Offertory and then in the other parts of the Mass. The congregation was reduced to silent witnessing of the actions of a priest speaking in a language that became increasingly foreign. People were then encouraged to see the Mass as an occasion for private, devotional meditation on Jesus' Passion and death and on their entering into the Passion and death.

This development in liturgy illustrates well how changes occur. The Church *intended* to stress moral development and life in imitation of the life of Christ. It did not originally intend to separate the priest from the people so radically nor to turn the corporate action of the liturgy into an occasion of private devotion. These latter results were the *unintended* but powerful and lasting consequences of the Church's attempts to meet the challenges posed by its new barbarian members.

The forces that shape our lives are almost always such a combination of intended and unintended developments. We are usually quite conscious of the developments that are intended, but we often overlook the unintended ones which are often more powerful. If we are to be the artists responsible for the creation of our own lives, we will need to be much more critically reflective on what is happening to us. We need the opportunities and ability to stand back from what is happening in our Church lives and to consider how even some laudable reforms may be taking us in directions that are not so desirable.

Parish That Shaped Us

One feature of the Church today is a massive wave of critical reflection as we try to correct what we see as pervasive institional*ism* in the Church. To oppose institutionalism is to recognize that some institutions or structures in the Church may actually be working against the purposes for which they are intended or may have become somewhat self-serving. Antiinstitutionalism takes the form of antidogmatism, anticlericalism, antiritualism, antitraditionalism, and antidevotionalism. To the extent that doctrinal teaching placed so much emphasis on compliance with orthodox formulations of faith that it neglected interior, personal development of faith, the teaching tended to place faith outside of us. It is this dogmat*ism*, not dogma, that we are trying to correct by relating faith more clearly to the experiences and expressions of people.

To the extent that the contribution of the priesthood to the Church tended to eclipse the priestly responsibility of all Christians and to suggest a special caste, the exercise of the priesthood then had the unintended effect of distancing priests from people and of minimizing the participation of people in the mission of the Church. It is this tendency to clerical*ism* that is undergoing reform.

The worship life of the Church can turn ritual into ritual*ism* when attention to certain external practices becomes so exaggerated as to minimize the significance of the *faith* we bring to worship or the *manner* in which we celebrate these rites. Simply performing some practice for a specified number of times can even appear to have a saving effect. It is this danger of ritual*ism* that we are trying to correct.

When tradition becomes less the roots of our present faith and Church life and more an iron cage from which we cannot escape, then the riches of tradition become the unquestionable burden of precedent. It is this traditional*ism* that we are attempting to reduce in the Church.

Finally, when, for a number of reasons, the devotional life of the Church becomes exaggerated in overly sentimental piety or takes precedence over the liturgy, we are caught in devotional*ism*. Much of the recent reform has been an attempt to restore the action of Christ in the liturgy to a central place in our spirituality.

The danger, of course, in antiinstitutionalism is that it can degenerate into a naively antiinstitutional attitude. Institutions are, after all, only the ways we ensure careful attention to those elements of our lives that are too important to be left to chance. We will always have institutions because we will always develop structures for ensuring care for what is important. The challenge is to monitor these structures so that they will neither become self-serving nor accidentally interfere with other important things.

I have been careful to lay out a context for our reflection on the parish of the past and the parish of the present because I think we have to look deeply into the patterns of Church life to see not only the obvious and intended patterns, but also the less evident and often unintended ones. It is only when we do this that we can truly assess the past and be responsible for the present and future. We also know that we will be establishing ways to carry on the life of the Church that will become standard, and we have to ensure that these structures are truly serving the mission of the Church as we come to understand that mission. With this in mind, let us review briefly some of the patterns of the parish of the past.

II. The Parish That Shaped Us

What were some of the *intended* shaping influences of the parish of the past?

The parish was a clear and determined teacher about the mystery of God, the redemptive action of Christ, and the importance of the Church for our salvation. We were taught about our radical sinfulness, but also about the availability of God's grace and forgiveness. There were clear prescriptions and rules governing our moral life and just as clear sanctions for violating these prescriptions. There were strong norms and plentiful forgiveness.

The sacraments of the Church were clear channels of God's grace. Furthermore, more than half the days of the year were assigned some religious meaning, forming a whole rhythm of time or environment reminding us of our obligations to God. These were Lent and Advent, holy days of obligation and Sundays, fast days and feast days, all Fridays and especially first Fridays. Special names of saints, special words used in the church, special practices such as ashes and abstinence: all tended to reinforce our identity as Catholics. These and many more actions, such as requirements for sacraments, schools and hospitals, parish missions, and the call to support the foreign missions, were clear and intended forces of formation.

There were also *unintended* forces of formation. The social condition of our largely poor, immigrant Catholics, regarded with suspicion and treated with discrimination by their fellow Americans, was a powerful force for solidarity and support for the influence of the Church. The education gap between priests and people reinforced the authority of the Church, as did Catholics' recourse to the parish for so many services besides strictly religious services. The view that outside the Church lay not only jeopardy to salvation but also dangers from anti-Catholics led us to have minimal demands for baptism, for we had to make this single source of salvation as available as possible. At the same time, attempts to prove that Catholics were just as American as others led to active adoption of the culture's values. We were just as likely to give special honor to those who were rich and powerful among us.

The fact that the Church ordered everything into hierarchies — ranking doctrines, moral obligations, offices in the Church, feasts, and Church structures — suggested a pervasive *order* to life but an order that was intimately interconnected. If any one part of the order collapsed, the whole order seemed to collapse.

Thus, the central character of Mary Gordon's book *Final Payments* remarks: "And when the church ceased to be inevitable, it became for me irrelevant. And then there was the Council with its sixties' relevance and relativity that interested me not a whit."[2]

The extent to which the parish shaped us depended on both these intentional and unintentional forces for formation. But it is important to recall how much we also endorsed formation by the values of the American society. If we regard with dismay how much we have internalized these values, we must recall that aspirants to any position tend to adopt the styles of that position in an exaggerated fashion. And we encouraged one another to aspire to American positions of success.

We cannot stop at this level in our search for the forces that formed us. We must look even more deeply into the life of the Church in the parish to discover some even more profound patterns of religious life that were encouraged by the parish. I would like to suggest that one way of understanding the basic orientation of parish life is to examine how it fostered *solidarity in suffering*.

Central to this solidarity was the value of suffering. Surely, a Church of largely poor people was a Church of considerable suffering. The life of the Church encouraged people to identify their suffering with the suffering of Christ and, therefore, to see that suffering could be redemptive. Not only did the parish not try to ignore suffering, but it constantly presented us with assertions of the importance of suffering. We who are old enough or imaginative enough can think of how much the imagery in the parish church confronted us with suffering: the realistic stations of the cross, the large crucifix with Christ in agony, the pictures of the Sacred Heart, and even the usually somber statues of Mary and the strong statue of a rugged Joseph ready for hard work. But, beyond this, there were encouragements to further hardship:

---

2. Mary Gordon, *Final Payments* (New York: Random House, 1978) 18.

Parish That Shaped Us

Lenten and Friday abstentions and fasts, financial sacrifice for the good of all in the Church, and services with much kneeling. The suffering and death of Jesus was regularly put before us in relation to our sins, especially in the periodic parish missions.

Suffering was not a cause for despondency or despair. Quite the contrary! It was not glamorized, but it was only by entering into our suffering and death that we could find freedom and salvation. Our limitations were constantly before us, but so also were the possibilities of grace, forgiveness, the help of God, and personal accomplishment. We had to acknowledge the shame of our sins and failings, but we walked out of the darkness of penance into the light of forgiveness and new confidence. Nor did the liturgy of the funeral make any attempt to veil the darkness of death; we were to face death without illusion. Heroism in facing the terror of death was presented to us in Jesus and Mary and Joseph, in the saints, and even in our understanding of the lives of priests and religious.

Suffering is a basic factor in religious life, as is reflection on those heroes who have been able to find and give meaning to their suffering, to find hope rather than despair in suffering. It is faith that enables people to give such meaning to the suffering that is inevitable in life. By entering into suffering in solidarity with Jesus and with one another, then, we were to find life. It is important for us to consider how much the parish shaped our religious lives by fostering this solidarity in suffering.

There were excesses in this approach to religious life, excesses which we might characterize as promoting uniformity in rejecting the human condition. Solidarity could be distorted into pressures to widespread uniformity in our religious lives, the kind of uniformity that ignores the differences among individuals or cultures. Moreover, attention to suffering could be distorted into a view that urged suffering for its own sake or that made any of the pleasures of human life indecent. Suffering was then no longer a necessary evil through which we must continually pass to life, but an end in itself.

In spite of distortions, the parish shaped us in very profound ways. It reached down into the heart of our uncertainty, into our fears and frailties, into the terror of death and the tragedy of suffering. The Church was no stranger to the dark side of life. This is what made people like Graham Greene and Flannery O'Connor *Catholic* writers: their confrontation with the dark forces of life, through which alone the light of grace could be seen in all its power. Furthermore, attention to suffering was very immediate and individual; it was not generalized. The emotion it evoked, to use a distinction by the political analyst Hannah Arendt, was *compassion* not concern. We have *compassion* when we face all the intensity of suffering of individual persons; we have *concern* when we see only generalized suffering of injustice.

Let us shift the scene now and look at some of the values encouraged by patterns of today's parish life.

III. Patterns of Renewal

It is much easier to acquire an overview of the past than to be accurate observers of our own time. There are numerous articles and books that attempt to give us some sense of the basic meaning of Vatican II and of the Church of the years since the Council. These writings have been helpful.

Recently Karl Rahner, S.J., has proposed that the fundamental interpretation of Vatican II is that it was, "in a rudimentary form still groping for identity, the Church's first official self-actualization *as* a world Church."[3] Observing that this was the first Council where native bishops represented all the cultures of the world, Rahner points out that this was a fundamental break from a Church seen as essentially a European Church located throughout the world. The Church, he further argues, is only beginning to experience the significance of its being a coming together of all the world's cultures.

3. Karl Rahner, "A Basic Interpretation of Vatican II," *Theological Studies* 40, no. 4 (1979) 717.

Surely, the multicultural self-understanding of the Church is part of a larger acknowledgement of pluralism in the Church. This pluralism can be found in every diocese and every parish. It is expressed not only in the different styles of parishes but even in the different styles of Sunday Masses in the same parish. This pluralism is described in the landmark book by Avery Dulles, S.J., *Models of the Church* (Garden City, N.Y.: Doubleday & Co., Inc., 1974). In this book, Dulles sketches the basically different viewpoints people have about the nature and purpose of the Church. The models that Dulles described can be identified in parishes we know. We have all seen parishes which embody what Dulles calls the "institutional" model of the Church. These are parishes with an emphasis on organized activities. They are highly structured parishes emphasizing clear lines of authority and clearly spelled out responsibility. They also emphasize providing services to people.

We have seen examples of Dulles' second model, the Church as "mystical communion." These are parishes which emphasize hospitality or which are deeply affected by the charismatic renewal. They are not so much concerned with providing services as with building fellowship. They provide opportunities for people to pray together and to enjoy one another's company or to care for one another. The priests or other staff are available for people when they want help. Liturgy in such parishes is characterized by a feeling of warmth and openness among the people.

The "Church-as-sacrament" model, Dulles' third model, is equally evident in parishes. These parishes place strong emphasis on the liturgy, on the sacraments, on liturgical spirituality. These parishes pay a great deal of attention to preparation for baptism, Communion, and marriage, trying to underscore the basic sacramental reality.

Dulles' fourth model, the "Church as herald," may be less prevalent, but it can be seen in parishes that focus their energies on promoting conversion, either among those who are not part of the Church, or even among those already participating in the parish. The preaching is very explicitly directed toward eliciting a response of faith rather than a response of understanding or of action. There are catechumenate programs and encounter weekends to foster conversion, or there are numerous attempts to reach out to people who are not members of the Church and to encourage them to consider the gospel of Jesus and life in the Church.

Finally, we have seen, to use Dulles' last model, "servant" parishes. These see their primary mission as promoting human development in any way. They are involved in social action programs, in coalitions, in encouraging people to take action to change their lives. They may wish that school children and their parents were more active in the worship life of the Church, but, in poor areas, they still find value in having parish schools that provide basic educational skills for the young. They are ecumenical and regard little in the way of human development as lying outside the scope of parish life.

These basic stances of parishes have enormous consequences for the kinds of religious life and understanding they generate. The existence of these various styles and our awareness of choosing one style or another are evidence of some of the pluralism of parish life.

Though styles of parish life may differ, still there are some basic directions (and lessons) for religious life that can be found in most parishes attempting to follow the lead of Vatican II. One lesson of current parish life is that the celebration of the liturgy must give evidence of the intimate connection between the action of Christ and the faith of the worshipers. The liturgy belongs to the people, who are to play an active role in the celebration of the liturgy. They are not to be spectators of something done for them, but participants in what is done. God's grace is assuredly available in the sacraments, but the liturgy as an event of grace requires the faith-filled participation of every person.

A second lesson of current parish life is that the sacred and secular aspects of life are intimately related. The sacred is not something apart from our secular lives. The altar is not distanced from us, but in our midst. It is not only the ordained who are to touch the Eucharist. Concerns of the world are not to be left outside the church but are to be incorporated into our worship and our reflection on the Scriptures. There are distinct functions in the Church, such as that of priest, but this does not mean that it is the priest alone who is responsible for the sacred dimensions of life. Rather, each person shares in some way in the priesthood of Jesus and is to attempt to bring out the sacred features of every part of life.

A third lesson is that responsibility for the mission of the Church belongs to all in the Church. The use of parish councils, rejection of the notion that the priest or sister is to take care of everything, and the underscoring of the ministerial responsibility of all express this collective responsibility for the mission of the Church.

A fourth lesson of the present parish is that the life of faith is not something firmly established once and for all in our youth. Rather, faith is a continuing challenge to increasingly adult commitment. Opportunities to reflect on our faith are more numerous; the new emphasis on the rite of Christian initiation for adults stresses the need for adult commitment; the transfer of confirmation to a later age is meant to provide an opportunity for more adult commitment to faith and to the life of the Church. Adult education is much talked about, though we must admit that it remains still relatively underdeveloped. But, in all these ways, we have acknowledged that assurance of the commitment of faith lies not only in care about the teaching of the Church but also in repeated opportunities for all of us to reflect deeply on the faith that moves us to action.

A fifth lesson of today's parish is that we have direct access to God. While the action of God is mediated to us through the Church and sacraments, we are each able to approach God, and God is acting in our lives in numerous ways.

Finally, a sixth lesson of today's parish is that God's action is not restricted to the Catholic Church. There is renewed awareness of God's action in other churches and new appreciation for the many ways people respond to the one God. This has had the result of considerable discussion about the special character of the Church. Once we acknowledged that there are many ways in which God acts and people respond, there grew a tendency to insist that membership in the Church requires a much deeper commitment to faith and to the life of the Church. This had led many parishes to become much more demanding about the conditions necessary for the reception of baptism and the other sacraments.

We may leave our review with these six lessons being communicated to us by the life of today's parish. Other people will think that there are further, and even more important, elements in the formation process of today's parish. This may well be true, but this short list gives us some hint of the formation intended by some of the developments in parish life.

My real concern in this presentation is not so much to identify the intentional and relatively obvious formation forces at work in today's parish because, in spite of these rich developments in the life of the parish in the past decade, we have to admit to a dim awareness that there is often a kind of hollowness to what we are doing. Beneath all the attempts to bring vitality to the parish and to give evidence of the Church's modern consciousness, we may have the nagging feeling that there remains something missing. Therefore, I would like to point to what appear to be unintentional and less examined directions or results of some of our practices. Because my impressions are somewhat tentative, I will generally use questions to make these points.

IV. Unintentional Parish Influences Today

First, as we encourage both preparation for baptism and the initiation of adults, are we sometimes suggesting that the Church is for the fully committed, not for the people struggling to believe and to be open to the life of God? In a survey among priests in New York parishes, we found that the most frequently mentioned purpose for baptism was entrance into the Christian community. Only secondly was entrance into the life of God mentioned. Certainly a significant function of baptism, must not entrance into the community nevertheless be seen as a means of entering into communion with the Lord?

Does the postponement of confirmation to a later age and the related suggestion that confirmation is for only those who are prepared to make the beginnings of mature commitment suggest that the sacrament is more an expression of the initiative of the individual than of the action of the Spirit?

Let us turn back to the example I used earlier from Gregory Dix regarding the Eucharist, turning his example upside down. There is a largely unspoken understanding that all present at Mass should take Communion and participate in all the activities of the Mass. Thus there is little or no personal reflection at Mass, other than attentiveness to the specific words said. This means that there is little encouragement to make contact with the Passion and death of Jesus and, I would suggest, the eucharistic acclamation that seems to fit least is the one that says: "When we eat this bread and drink this cup, we proclaim your death, Lord Jesus, until you come in glory." Finally, are we implying that all people are in a condition or state once unfortunately said to be true of the diocesan priest, namely, a state of acquired perfection? An old distinction made between the diocesan priest and one in a religious order was that while the religious life was a way of acquiring perfection through the common exercise of the counsels of poverty, chastity, and obedience, the diocesan priest was in a state of already acquired perfection from which he ministered to others. As I said, this was an unfortunate formulation regarding the priest. Are we now suggesting that of all Christians?

In the rite of reconciliation, the revision was intended in part to underscore the communal character of sin and forgiveness. Do we not, in fact, lessen that communal aspect because relatively few actually have to acknowledge failure to another person except in the most anonymous and undifferentiated ways? Furthermore, to the extent that we promote the communal rite, are we not also putting the priest in a situation where he has only the most generic concern about the struggle of Christian living, rather than the compassion that comes from sharing the struggles of individual people? Finally, given the tendency for the individual rite to suggest that the priest is engaged in spiritual counselling, are we implying that all priests are equally able to be directors of souls?

In the anointing of the sick, the parish tends to be less involved in anointing at the moment of death because so many people die in hospitals or nursing homes. The communal rite is meant to embrace people in varying conditions of sickness or advanced age. Does this change also make the rite much less directly tied to the terror of death and the related grace of God? Moreover, in the funeral rite, has the emphasis on the resurrection made less likely our encounter with the darkness of death? Has the frequent, though prohibited, turning of the homily into a eulogy further stressed so much the goodness of all that we avoid the mystery of our sinfulness and limitations?

Has one result of *Humanae vitae* been so to silence priests about the whole area of sexuality and birth that the Church does not deal with the awesome decisions people face regarding life and the extension of their own lives beyond their deaths? Has the popularizing of psychology as a framework for pastoral counselling brought with it the notion that salvation comes from self-knowledge alone? Has the change of Lent to emphasize what we may do for others, rather than sacrificial confrontation with our own weaknesses and need for self-control, robbed us of an opportunity to face the weaknesses and limitations in us that are intimations of our mortality?

Some of these lessons implicit in current pastoral practice may be summarized in terms of a few basic directions which the formation process of parish life seems to be taking today.

First, we may be encouraging a kind of optimistic idealism as a fundamental stance of the Christian. Karl Rahner asserts that "pessimistic realism" is the basic stance of Christians because they are regularly aware of their own death and of their weaknesses and limitations. I am not sure that "pessimistic" is a good word for what Rahner describes, but we may be implying the opposite, namely, that we are all capable of the most Christian of lives all the time. We avoid notions of personal guilt and failure, weaknesses, and the ever present seeds of death in our lives.

Second, then, we may be sharing our culture's denial of death. We may have so turned away from facing the reality of Jesus' death and our own death — our final death and the many deaths we must pass through in the course of our lives — that we are reducing the possibility of seeing Christ and the Church as life-giving.

Third, we may be subtly adopting a kind of romanticism in our approach to ministry. This occurs when we suggest that all are equally called to ministry or that every feeling of a call warrants opportunity to exercise ministry. This seems to fly in the face of psychological studies that point to the stages of human development and our unevenness in moving through these stages, or studies in spirituality that say the same thing about stages of spiritual development. Romanticism also occurs when we blithely suggest that we are all capable of some intimate Christian community as a normal character of our relationships. It occurs further when our approach to social action is to move to the level of ideology or to concern for the distant hungry rather than the suffering going on near us.

To the extent that these implications are found in our ministry, I suggest that our intention of bringing the life of the Church in the parish much closer to people's lives may unintentionally be having precisely the opposite effect. We may be making the Church more remote, not because our approaches to activities in the Church are not familiar, for they are. But we make the world of the Church more remote from the worlds of people's families and neighborhoods and work if the world of our religious symbols does not acknowledge the struggles and sinfulness of life, the terror of death, and the difficulty of truly Christian relationships.

One way of summarizing a basic approach of the present parish as a shaping influence on Christian life is to say that the parish stresses *plurality and power*. It stresses plurality in the many options in individual rites, in styles of parish, and even in approaches of individuals to Christian life. Implicit also may be an emphasis on the power that each person has. We may do this by reducing the power differences between clergy and laity, by emphasizing the priesthood of all believers, by underscoring the individual's access to God, by displaying crucifixes that portray Christ as the confident and crowned high priest, by removing the realistic stations, by statues of Mary and Joseph in the understated colors and slender forms of wealth refinement, by emphasizing the power—however much grace oriented—we bring to the sacraments of baptism and confirmation, and by suggesting that we are capable of extraordinary forms of Christian life and relationships with one another.

In the extreme, this emphasis turns into an endorsement of a kind of idiosyncratic worth of every person, position, and reform. Then we move from pluralism to a kind of atomization of all the individuals of the Church as relatively self-sufficient. We face, then, an inability to test the worth of either Christian lives or individual interpretations of Christian responsibility. We can arrive at the stage where everyone can design a liturgy; everyone is equally capable of ministering; all theologies are of equal value; no one should be a leader of others; all are capable of well-formed consciences. As I said, this is the extreme of the position of plurality and power. But in the extreme, we shun shame and guilt and avoid whatever bespeaks our weaknesses, our fallibility, our frailty, and our mortality.

There are some striking exceptions to what I have said — pastoral developments which quite clearly take on the mystery of suffering and death. Let me cite a few of these.

One of the most prolific developments in pastoral ministry has been the ministry to divorced Catholics. In its best form, this ministry involves the parish in helping people to enter into all the aspects of the death of their marriages. The suffering of separation is not to be avoided but to be entered into with the assistance of others and the aid of God's grace, so that the building of a new life is not a construction on sand, which is what would occur if people tried simply to put aside the suffering of divorce.

A further development in pastoral ministry has been an increase in ministry to the poorest of the poor. These are often the street people who are not reached by our social agencies, or people like migrant workers who live in the most desperate of conditions. They may be the deinstitutionalized mental patients, the chemically dependent, the shopping-bag ladies. Ministry to these brothers and sisters has moved many people beyond the clinical work of agencies to the specific and often helpless sufferings of individual people, beyond concern about suffering to compassion with those who are suffering.

The emergence of base communities or any of their variants has had dramatic consequences for the religious lives of those involved. Typically, these are small groups of people who attempt to be keenly self-conscious regarding what is happening in their individual lives and in the lives of their communities. They confront these problems directly, avoiding the temptation to isolate themselves from difficulties through continual gratification or distraction. And they know that although they must struggle to change things, they will be only partially successful at best.

Similarly, the many parishes that have become involved in communitiy organizing have come to know the struggles and limitations of bringing about change. They come to realize not only the injustices in society but the ways we all are accomplices in these injustices, and yet they fight on to initiate change. They know that the very process of struggling together changes the meaning of their problems.

Also, growing ministry to the dying, either in individual instances or through hospice programs, has put many people in touch with the questions and the mystery of death.

Ministry to faith is also growing: explicit attempts to have people examine their faith candidly, acknowledging both where their faith is strong and where there are serious doubts.

There are many other instances of ministry that touch the most basic mysteries of life. What is true of the forms I have mentioned is: first, they enable people to confront the struggles they are having; second, they do so by enabling people, in most instances, to minister to one another; third, they recognize that there are severe limits to what can be changed and that our future partly depends on living with what cannot be changed; fourth, they remind us that we will continue to carry within us the marks of our own failure and that we are often accomplices in our own suffering; and fifth, they recall that the ministry of the Church is not for the healthy but for those who need healing, not for those who have already achieved a sure direction for their lives but for all of us who continually need the peace and confidence that only the Lord can give.

V. Directions for Change

It would be foolish for me to attempt to suggest how we might preserve all the advantages of present developments in the Church while correcting all the unintended consequences. The best I can do is to indicate some obstacles that we may need to overcome.

We may, first, need to ensure that there are no unreasonable limitations on the power that people can have in the Church before we can talk about the reasonable limitations on all of us. Because we still prevent people from taking part in the ministry of the parish for reasons that are no longer credible — thus preventing them from sharing responsibility in the parish — we may inadvertently encourage the notion that no one who would be responsible for Church ministry need be accountable to the Church.

Second, while proposing strong ideals for all members of the Church, we may need to distinguish this goal from requirements for entrance into the Church. It may require a revitalized celebration of the sacrament of reconciliation before we can acknowledge our own sinfulness sufficiently well to make us reluctant to exclude others from access to the grace of God mediated through the Church.

Third, we must be more clear in talking about all the mysteries of life and death, the mysteries of sexuality and life and the darkness of death. If we do not deal with death, we do not need faith. This applies to all the shortcomings and frailties we have. In fact, although there is much discussion suggesting that the hollowness referred to earlier as characteristic of otherwise vital parishes is symptomatic of a failure to come to grips with very basic questions of faith, the real failure in the first instance may be our not coming to grips with the suffering and death that is in the life of each of us.

Fourth, we may say that any parish ministry that does not make clear our responsibility for all who are poor or powerless is not only inauthentic but futile.

Finally, our parishes must face the struggle endemic to modern life, the struggle to fashion our own existence. This is something that we all appreciate, clergy and laity, men and women alike. For we all face the challenge to form what it means to be a person and a believer, a priest or a parent, a citizen or a worker. Karl Rahner suggests that the pluralism implied in this challenge is inevitable. Raimundo Panikkar stresses the same point and urges that we have moved from the question "What is man?" and the question "Who am I?" to the question "Who are you?" His point is that we will fashion our lives adequately only when we try to understand the others whose lives touch on and affect ours. Great anxiety is associated with realizing the burden of shaping our own lives, and the Church must minister to this struggle.

We are shaping ourselves and the next generation of Catholics in the parish of today. We have the capacity to be much more self-conscious about the kinds of formation we intend and the kinds of influences we are unintentionally having. We need to examine both very carefully.

In closing, let me turn to a reflection on those who try to carry out God's mission and whose shape may not always have been evident. Wallace Stevens talks of this in his short poem "The Good Man Has No Shape."

> Through centuries he lived in poverty,
> God only was his only elegance.
>
> Then generation by generation he grew
> Stronger and freer, a little better off.
>
> He lived each life because, if it was bad,
> He said a good life would be possible.
>
> At last the good life came, good sleep, bright fruit,
> And Lazarus betrayed him to the rest,
>
> Who killed him, sticking feathers in his flesh
> To mock him. They placed with him in his grave
>
> Sour wine to warm him, an empty book to read,
> And over it they set a jagged sign,
>
> Epitaphium to his death, which read,
> The Good Man Has No Shape, as if they knew.[4]

4. From *The Collected Poems of Wallace Stevens* by Wallace Stevens. Copyright © 1947 by Wallace Stevens. Reprinted by permission of Alfred A. Knopf, Inc.

The Parish in the American Past

JAY DOLAN AND JEFFREY BURNS

For the historian interested in studying the religion of the people, the parish community is the place to begin. This is where the historian will encounter the ordinary, common folk and discover what religion meant in the everyday lives of people. Unfortunately, it is much easier said than done. To pursue such a study historically takes a great deal of time, and frustration can mount very rapidly because of the disparate nature of the sources as well as their scarcity. But if we are ever going to penetrate the hidden past of the American Catholic community and uncover the meaning of religion at the grass roots, then the focus of our attention must be the parish.

Before undertaking a study of the parish, the historian must realize that this institution has changed over time. The parish as we know it today had its beginnings in the sixteenth century when the Council of Trent reorganized and renewed Catholic life. Prior to Trent, the parish was not the vital center for the religion of the people. After the Council, the parish became a key component in religious renewal, and it gradually became

---

JAY DOLAN is an associate professor of history at the University of Notre Dame and director of the Cushwa Center for the Study of American Catholicism. He is author of *The Immigrant Church* and *Catholic Revivalism*.

JEFFREY BURNS is research and administrative assistant at the Cushwa Center for the Study of American Catholicism at the University of Notre Dame.

more and more uniform and standardized throughout the Catholic world. Despite such uniformity in parish organization during the last four hundred years, diverse types of parishes, reflecting various cultures and styles of piety, have emerged. A rural parish in seventeenth-century France was light years away from a nineteenth-century parish in the city of Paris; in the United States a parish community in 1800 differed considerably from its heir in the twentieth century. The task of the historian is to seek to understand this change and be able to explain it. This essay, then, will examine the development of the parish in the United States and offer a historical typology of parish organization so that, in understanding the past, we may acquire a more enlightened view of the present.

I. The Congregational Parish

In the first stage of parish development, roughly from 1760 to 1860, one type of parish stood out. This type can be called the congregational parish. I have chosen this label because the term congregational emphasizes two trends which were dominant in this early period of American Catholic history. The first is the emphasis on a democratic model of authority rather than a hierarchical model; the second trend suggested by the term congregational is the emphasis on local autonomy, where the relationship to authority beyond the local level is poorly defined and only minimally actualized.

Prior to the mid-eighteenth century, colonial Catholicism was not organized around parish communities. Among Maryland Catholics, religion was centered in the home and performed privately in the community of the family. This was the tradition of English Catholicism during the seventeenth century, and it was carried over to the New World by the Catholic gentry who migrated to Maryland. Only in the 1760s, after anti-Catholic tensions subsided, did the Maryland Catholic community begin to establish parishes. In Pennsylvania, a similar development took place in Philadelphia, Lancaster, and other more rural villages. The striking point in this early phase of Catholic history is not the absence of the parish, but the decidedly domestic and private nature of religion. Once parishes began to be established at the Jesuit farms and mission centers, the Church not only became more identified with a specific locale, but the exercise of religion also became more public and more congregational. Parish records and sacramental records now began to appear with faithful regularity and in scrupulous detail; liturgy was performed publicly in a parish setting, and the rites of passage also began to take place at the parish church. Devotional societies soon emerged, and a definite sense of parochial community was evident.

These first parishes in Maryland and Pennsylvania were rather traditional, European-style parishes which emphasized territorial organization, hierarchical authority, and sacerdotal supremacy. This was the type of parish which developed from the reform movement of the Council of Trent, and it became the normative model in the Roman Catholic world. Clearly it did not fit the model of the congregational parish at all. But these traditional types of parishes, organized and staffed by the Jesuits, and modeled after a European prototype, did not set the pattern for parish development after the Revolution. What emerged after the American Revolution and remained dominant into the early nineteenth century was the congregational parish — a model that was strikingly American principally because of its emphasis on a republican style of organization and government.

The reason for singling out the congregational parish as the dominant model in this first stage of development was the prevalance of the trustee system throughout the American Catholic community. As Patrick Carey has written, "The trustee movement permeated the American Catholic experience in the years immediately following the American Revolution." Since it "arose as a response to American conditions, it is no wonder that it developed in almost every major city and parish in the United States, from New York to Charleston to New Orleans."[1]

The trustee system of parish government was rooted in the democratic concept of election and representation. Basically it meant that the people of the parish, generally those who rented seats in the church, would annually elect a board of trustees. This board would govern the affairs of the parish, in principle confiding its interests to temporal issues, but often in practice involving itself in spiritual, pastoral concerns as well. As Carey has pointed out, the reasons for the spread of the trustee system and the emergence of the congregational parish were numerous: immigration and the presence of national differences among the Irish, Germans, and French; the diaspora condition of American Catholicism, in which there were few clergy; and an absence of an elaborated diocesan organizational structure. A general acceptance of the democratic political ideology was another major contributing factor, but as Carey noted, "The primary force behind the movement was the trustees' own theological perceptions of the Church and its relationship to society."[2]

Carey has thoroughly examined this phenomenon, and it is evident from his writings that the trustee system and the congregational parish which it fostered were much more widespread and accepted than historians have previously acknowledged. Though the American hierarchy attempted to legislate against this development in 1829, it remained a popular model of parish organization through the 1850s. In Cincinnati, for example, as late as 1851, Bishop Purcell issued regulations concerning the activities of the trustees in the German parishes of his diocese. In 1865, he again issued similar regulations and stated that "without extending the system where it is neither necessary nor desired, we approve of it where it does exist." Purcell not only officially approved of the system, but applauded the "quiet,

1. Patrick Carey, "The Laity's Understanding of the Trustee System, 1785-1855," *Catholic Historical Review* 64 (July 1978) 358.
2. *Ibid.* 372.

orderly, efficient and edifying spirit and manner with which lay counsellors, wherever employed in this Archdiocese, cooperate with the Pastor in attending to their duties."[3]

A computer-assisted study of parishes in Illinois and Kentucky offered some suggestive data as regards the rise and decline of the congregational parish.[4] Prior to the 1860s in Illinois, 53 percent of the parishes founded had trustees; the same trend persisted through the 1870s, and then it changed significantly, with only one in four parishes choosing this option in the last decades of the nineteenth century. Though the figures do not tell us how elaborate the concept of trusteeism was in these parishes, they do suggest that the trend toward trusteeism underwent a significant decline in the closing decades of the nineteenth century, and this continued into the first two decades of the twentieth century, when only 18 percent of the parishes founded had some vestige of trusteeism.

These figures from the parish history sample are more suggestive than definitive; all they really indicate is that the concept of trusteeism, either with an elaborated political and theological ideology as its base or simply as a perfunctory administrative system, was in vogue prior to the 1870s. The studies of Carey and others suggest that it was the dominant model of parish organization up until the 1830s, and, though it underwent a decline in later years, it remained a possible and popular option through the 1860s.

II. The Devotional Parish

The second type of parish to develop in the Catholic community was the devotional parish. This began to emerge slowly in the

---

3. Joseph White, "Religion and Community: Cincinnati Germans 1814–1870" (Unpublished Ph.D. dissertation, University of Notre Dame, 1980) 215.

4. This study, based on a parish history collection at the University of Notre Dame and conducted by Jeffrey Burns, examined 88 parishes in Illinois and 24 in Kentucky.

years preceding 1870, and then it quickly became the most popular and widespread type of parish up until the 1950s.

Prior to the 1870s, the traditional European-style parish based on territorial organization, a hierarchical mode of government, and a sacerdotal monopoly, certainly did exist. It was the normative model of parish in post-Tridentine Roman Catholicism, but in the United States it was not very pervasive in the early nineteenth century because of the popularity of the congregational parish. Because of efforts by the lay trustees to extend their authority to areas that were traditionally the domain of the clergy, and also because of an increased concern on the part of the bishops and priests for more control over church affairs, the trustee system fell into disfavor among the hierarchy, and every effort was employed to abolish it. Though such efforts were never totally successful, it was clear that the age of the congregational parish was over. Thus, as the congregational parish became less and less normative, the traditional European parish, or what can be called the Tridentine parish, became the more accepted model for the organization of local Catholic communities. After 1870, however, this type of parish took on a new ingredient which was so striking that it became the trademark of the Tridentine parish in the nineteenth and early twentieth centuries. This new ingredient was the presence of devotional societies. The evidence for this is so overwhelming that it cannot be ignored or accepted as merely suggestive.

The parish history study revealed that the Illinois parishes founded 425 societies or groups; half of these (51 percent — 218) were devotional societies. That in itself is striking, but it becomes even more so when it is seen that the second and third most popular type of society, namely, the charitable and mutual aid societies, represented only 11 percent and 10 percent, respectively, of the societies founded. The same pattern holds true for the parishes studied in Kentucky. Breaking these figures down according to their founding date, it also is evident that this type of society emerged only after 1860. In the Illinois group studied, thirty-two parishes were founded prior to 1860, but there were only twelve devotional societies established; in other words, the bulk of the devotional societies came into existence after 1860, especially in the 1860-1890 period.

The principal reason for this shift is quite clear. Roman Catholicism was undergoing a devotional revolution in the second half of the nineteenth century, and this devotionalism became centered in the parish, where it was promoted and nurtured to an extraordinary degree.[5] The restoration and intensification of papal authority during the pontificate of Pius IX, the emergence of an elaborated diocesan organization in the United States which solidified episcopal authority, together with a corresponding demise of democratic ideology in Catholic ecclesiology, had led to the acceptance of the Tridentine parish as the chosen model for parochial organization. This was not a new model but simply the restoration of the traditional European parish. What was new was the extent to which this type of parish, based on territorial organization, hierarchical authority, and sacerdotal monopoly, became the center of an elaborate network of devotional societies.

Indeed this was the era of the immigrant church, and a claim could be made that the national parish or the ethnic parish was the dominant model. But, what all this says is that parishes were organized along national, ethnic lines and were very much identified with ethnic neighborhoods. Certainly this is a significant point and helps to explain the success of the Church in ministering to a plurality of ethnic groups. But was there a feature common to these ethnically diverse parishes that points to something other than ethnicity and more accurately defines the type of parish that emerged during the age of the immigrant church? Indeed there was; it was the widespread tendency to establish an

---

5. See Jay P. Dolan, *Catholic Revivalism: The American Experience 1830-1900* (Notre Dame, 1978) 32-33 for a discussion of this devotional revolution in the United States.

elaborate devotional network, and it was common to all parish communities, regardless of their ethnic makeup.

In every parish studied, regardless of its ethnicity, a devotional society was far and away the most popular form of organization. Among ethnic groups, however, there was one noticeable pattern of differentiation. In those parishes rooted in a foreign language tradition, chiefly the German and Polish, the predominance of devotional societies was greater than in parishes designated as Irish or American. This pattern would have to be studied further by including more parishes in the sample before it could be substantiated. As regards ethnicity, however, one pattern does come across very strongly, namely, the disinclination of the Irish to promote parish organizations. Though the Irish parishes made up 22 percent of the parishes studied, they accounted for only 14 percent of all the societies founded by these parishes. In every other group, the percent of societies was at least equal to or greater than that particular group's share of the sample study. Significantly, with the Irish as with every other group, the devotional type of society was overwhelmingly the most popular type of group founded.[6] In other words, of all groups, the Irish were less inclined to establish parish organizations; but of those organizations they did establish, the devotional society was far and away the most popular choice.

Another option is to label this the age of the organizational parish, that is, the parish distinguished by a multitude of voluntary societies and confraternities. But this also is too general a classification. The immediate question is what type of organization predominated, and the data overwhelmingly indicates that it was the devotional society; thus the choice of the term "devo-

---

6. The absence of an elaborate associational or organizational network in the Irish parishes is a phenomenon I encountered earlier in my study of Irish Catholics in New York; see Jay P. Dolan, "Immigrants in the City: New York's Irish and German Catholics," *Church History* 41 (September 1972) 360-61.

tional parish" to describe the dominant model to emerge in the second half of the nineteenth century.

Another feature of the devotional parish emerged from the analysis of the Illinois and Kentucky parishes — they were predominantly adult centered. Few organizations were established for children in their teens or younger; only one in five (23 percent) was in this category. Again, the most popular type of children's organization was the devotional society. As regards the establishment of parochial schools, definite patterns also emerged. The most noticeable was the reluctance of the nineteenth-century Irish to found a school shortly after the organization of the parish. Generally it took at least five years, and in most instances ten years or more, before the Irish parishes organized a parochial school. With the nineteenth-century Germans and Polish, however, schools were founded very soon after the organization of the parish, the vast majority within five years. In the twentieth-century, however, there was a striking difference; all groups, regardless of ethnic background, founded a school shortly after they organized a parish.

The devotional parish endured through the 1940s; parish missions periodically revived the spirit of the people and renewed the parish's commitment to devotionalism; novenas became increasingly popular, and they too reinforced the devotional aspect of parish life. New types of societies began to appear, chiefly organizations with an instructional focus, and others with a social or recreational emphasis, but the devotional character of the parish remained dominant.

III. The Voluntary Parish

Sometime after 1950 or so, certainly by the 1960s, the devotional type of parish began to disintegrate, and the Catholic parish entered a new stage of development. The first thing to go was the elaborate devotional network; obviously it did not happen overnight, but by the mid-1960s the devotional network, born in the late nineteenth century, was on its last legs. A principal reason for this, though not the only one, was the liturgical movement with its emphasis on a piety rooted in the liturgy and the Scriptures. Another reason was that Catholic devotionalism, or what Flannery O'Connor called the novena-rosary type of Catholicism, had became routinized and unsatisfying to many Catholics of the post–World War II era. For many, Catholic devotionalism had disintegrated into "observation without piety." The demise of the old-style devotionalism naturally reinforced the movement toward a new liturgical-scriptural piety.

Other features of the traditional parish also began to disintegrate. The territorial base became less important to people as they began to adopt the consumer mentality of shopping around for the best parish. The hierarchical, authoritarian structure changed and, though it has hardly vanished, many parishes have adopted a more democratic model of authority, with lay people and clergy working together in the administration of the parish. As this developed, sacerdotal supremacy also gave way. Obviously, there was a theological base for all of this. Just as a certain type of ecclesiology supported the emergence of the congregational parish and later a different ecclesiology promoted the concept of the devotional parish, so too a new theology of Church, of laity, and of ministry naturally led to a new model or type of parish. Moreover, the decades since World War II have witnessed the middle classification of American Catholics as they gradually became more like the rest of society economically, educationally, and culturally. This social and cultural change has reinforced the move away from the novena-rosary brand of old-time Catholicism.

What has emerged as a result of these social and religious changes is a new type of phenomenon as regards the parish. The parish now has become a radically voluntary institution. No one type or model dominates the landscape; a variety of parish types exists, just as different theologies of the Church exist, and Catholics are inclined to select the one that most suits their needs and tastes. For the lack of a better label, the post-Vatican II period can be called the age of the voluntary parish.

Religion is rooted in the voluntary choice of the individual. In the first and second stage of parish development, religion was clearly voluntary, and parish affiliation was certainly a freewill choice. But in seeking to single out the dominant ethos of the parish over the course of time, emphasis was placed on certain features that best described the prevailing model of parish. In the first stage of development, *polity* appeared to be the distinguishing feature (namely, the emphasis on a democratic form of government); in the second stage, *piety* was the chief characteristic (namely, the emphasis on devotionalism); and in the third stage, *pluralism* emerges as the dominant feature. This pluralism is rooted in the radically voluntary nature of religion which has developed in the last twenty years within the American Catholic community. The "republican ideals" endorsed by the American Revolution greatly influenced the first stage of parish development; the devotional revolution of nineteenth-century Roman Catholicism helped to explain the second stage; and the emphasis on individual religious freedom is a root cause for the emergence of voluntarism in contemporary Catholic parish life.

To say that the voluntary parish is the dominant contemporary model is only to affirm what theologians and sociologists have been saying for some time.[7] What is significant from the historical perspective is not so much the type of parish that has emerged in our own time as the change that the parish has undergone throughout history. To state that there is a new model of parish operative today obviously suggests change, and this is the key point. The parish has changed during the brief history of the American Catholic community, and this is to be

---

7. Philip J. Murnion offers a useful summary of the voluntary parish phenomenon in his essay *Forming the Parish Community* (Washington, D.C., 1978).

expected. Certainly this does not mean that the parish is dying or losing its effectiveness; it is simply changing to meet the needs of a changing community of faith. For some, the old-style devotional parish still remains the best model; for others, a parish rooted in an egalitarian style of operation is especially attractive; and for still others, a parish rooted in an intense commitment to evangelical, charismatic piety remains the chosen model. Other types, as well, claim the allegiance of people. What is significant in this current stage of parish development is the absence of any dominant model or type. Just as there are many mansions in God's kingdom, today more than ever before there are many different types of parishes in the American Catholic community. Religious diversity has emerged as the most visible and significant development in contemporary American Catholicism, and, not surprisingly, it has substantially altered the organization of parish communities.

II. ISSUES IN PARISH WORSHIP

The Sense of the Sacred

NATHAN MITCHELL, O.S.B.

It is commonly recognized that the passage of time brings not only healing but also the reassessment of persons and events, of private memories and public movements. Time has even a way of transforming villains into heroes and tragedies into triumph. Whether it is called "historical distance" or "revisionist history," it is a common experience that time has the power to bring about a change of perspective concerning what happened and why it should have happened. Today, for example, Abraham Lincoln's "Gettysburg Address" is generally admired for its sensitivity to the outrage of war and even for its remarkably effective prose style; yet when it was delivered in 1863, the speech received poor reviews. The *Chicago Times*, for instance, wrote:

> We did not conceive it possible that even Mr. Lincoln would produce a paper so slipshod, so loose-jointed, so puerile, not alone in literary construction, but in its ideas, its sentiments, its grasp. He has outdone himself. He has literally come out of the little end of his own horn. By the side of it, mediocrity is superb.[1]

No one today thinks of Lincoln's address as slipshod or puerile; on the contrary, it is regarded as the testament of a martyred

---

1. Cited in Nancy McPhee, *The Book of Insults* (New York: St. Martin's Press, 1978) 121.

NATHAN MITCHELL is a monk of St. Meinrad Archabbey, Indiana. He holds a doctorate in liturgy from the University of Notre Dame and is a professor of liturgy at St. Meinrad's Seminary. He is widely known as an author and lecturer.

president who spent himself for the sake of preserving the Union, of a man immortalized by Walt Whitman's poem "When Lilacs Last in the Dooryard Bloom'd."

Or, to take another example, when Jesus of Nazareth was executed, his death provoked an immediate devastation among his disciples. For one thing, Jewish tradition held no place for a martyred Messiah; on the contrary, "cursed is every man who hangs on a tree" (Deut 21:23; Gal 3:13). To complicate matters, Jesus' closest disciples had failed and fled; they had abandoned their Master at a moment of supreme crisis. With the passage of time, however, Jesus' death — and the disciples' failure — came to be regarded not as a disaster but as the holy martyrdom of God's holy prophet; as a fulfillment of God's plan for saving humankind; as the ultimate expiatory sacrifice that liberated men and women from that condition of human hostility towards God known as "sin." By the end of the first century A.D., the community associated with St. John's Gospel could speak of Jesus as the pre-existent Word of God who freely embraced his own death, fully conscious of his oneness with the Father, fully aware of what was happening to him and why.

Both these examples indicate how emphatically the passage of time changes our perception of people and events. They show us that history is not primarily an objective record of the past, but a continuing process of interpretation. We deal with the past not merely by recording it, but by assessing its meaning in the light of our present experience and of our hopes for the future. Though the two examples I have given are decisively different (at least for Christians), their relation to the process of interpretation is similar: "history" has transformed Lincoln from an embattled nineteenth-century politician into a national martyr, complete with cult and shrine; "history" has transformed Jesus from a religious prophet of doubtful reputation into the Risen One confessed by Christians as God's unique Son.

Time not only alters our perception and interpretation of people; it also provokes a reassessment of deeds and events.

Today, for instance, the liturgical movement and its influence on the reforms of the Second Vatican Council are coming in for critical reassessment. Postconciliar euphoria has given way to what, to many, seems an atmosphere of papal retrenchment. Others, of course, offer a different interpretation: irresponsible liturgical experimentation is being curtailed by responsible Roman leadership. It all depends which newspapers one chooses to read.

In any case, there is one criticism of the revised liturgy which keeps surfacing from both the left and the right. That criticism concerns the apparent loss of a "sense of the sacred" in the way Roman Catholics worship. The extreme right identifies this loss with the demise of the Latin language, Tridentine ritual, Gregorian chant, and Renaissance polyphony. The left argues that Christianity revolutionized the sense of the sacred, that Jesus liberated the sacred from the merely conventional, the holy from the purely cultic, God from human custom and law. Despite such apparently irreconcilable differences, however, traditionalists and liberals share one crucial conviction: both of them assume that a community's worship is the ordinary place where a sense of the sacred is mediated, felt, and affirmed. In this, even the most rawboned liberal is a traditionalist, a conservative convinced that Christianity's historical institutions and sacramental rites should be taken seriously.

A community's worship is the ordinary place where a sense of the sacred is mediated, felt, and affirmed: that is a conviction shared by people as diverse as Marcel Lefebvre and Karl Rahner, John Paul II and Hans Küng. This connection between liturgy and the sense of the sacred is rooted, I believe, in the experience of New Testament Christians. If we consider the resurrection appearance stories, particularly those found in Luke and John, we shall observe that although these stories stem from several different sources, they consistently make a connection between the appearance of the Risen One and the gathering of the disciples in a ritual context of meal and food. The Emmaus story begins on the road and ends at table, where Jesus, the stranger, reveals himself in the breaking of bread. On the shore of the Sea of Tiberius, Jesus the stranger prepares a breakfast of bread and fish — and the disciples knew it was the Lord (John 21:1-14). These stories combine elements of estrangement and recognition, divine initiative and human response — all clustered around the ritual symbol of meal. In the earliest decades of Christianity, the meal had already become a focal point through which a sense of the sacred, the presence of the Risen One, was mediated, felt, and affirmed. Ever since then, Christians have consistently returned to those familiar ritual patterns of food, drink, and meal as the sacred time and space for meeting the Holy One.

Rituals mediate the sacred; liturgy articulates people's sense of "holy presence." That is what Christians traditionally believe; that is what anthropologists who study archaic cultures tell us; that is even what psychologists like Erik Erikson are prepared to admit. But that is not what contemporary American culture tells us. Ours is a culture deeply and increasingly estranged from ritual. Notice, estranged from *ritual*, not estranged from *religion*. As a matter of fact, Americans are a fanatically religious people; our sense of the sacred is pervasive, not to say malignant. Consider the spiritual supermarkets of the west coast. Where else but in California could a twenty-million-dollar glass church be built, complete with drive-in facilities for worshipers who prefer to remain in their cars? Where else would someone like Beverly Sills be found to sing Schubert's "Ave Maria" at the dedication of such a church? We have the best religion money can buy!

But religion is one thing and ritual is another. We have a national religion whose name is therapy, whose priests are surgeons and analysts, whose strategy is to teach personal survival in an age whose social, economic, and political life seems to have run amok. In the final analysis, it is not the teaching of Christianity nor the findings of anthropologists nor the insights of psychologists which inform our society, but the pervasive influence of its general culture. And that culture is one which has a religion but lacks a rite.

Perhaps the problem could be stated slightly differently by saying that in our culture the connection between religion and ritual has been severed. The precincts of public ritual are no longer the forum where the sacred is sensed or encountered. In popular American culture, the sense of the sacred is something private, personal, interior, and intimate; the sacred is closely attached to the *self*, not to rituals celebrated and shared in public. Ritual has become a forgotten way of doing things; its power to mediate the sacred is, consequently, diminished.

Such, in brief, is the problem we are facing: the separation of religion from ritual and the corresponding attachment of the sacred to the private precincts of the self. This brings us to three issues for our consideration. First, we shall reflect upon the alleged loss of the sense of the sacred insofar as this affects liturgical reform and renewal. Second, we shall attempt to explore how and why the problem has developed. Third, we shall suggest how the sense of the sacred may be recovered within the context of Christian worship.

I. The Problem: Loss of a Sense of the Sacred

> The decay or perversion of ritual does not create an indifferent emptiness, but a void with explosive possibilities. . . . [Perhaps this] explains why "nice" people who have lost the gift of imparting values by meaningful ritualization can have children who become [or behave like] juvenile deliquents; and why nice "churchgoing" nations can so act as to arouse the impression of harboring pervasive murderous intent.[2]

These haunting words of Erik Erikson are quite enough to dampen the enthusiasm of even the most optimistic liturgist, but Erving Goffman goes even further:

---

2. Cited in Roland Delattre, "Ritual Resourcefulness and Cultural Pluralism," *Soundings* 51, no. 3 (Fall 1978) 286.

In contemporary society rituals performed to stand-ins for supernatural entities are everywhere in decay, as are extensive ceremonial agendas involving long strings of obligatory rites. What remains are brief rituals one individual performs for and to another, attesting to civility and good will on the performer's part and to the recipient's possession of a small patrimony of sacredness. What remains, in brief, are interpersonal rituals. These little pieties are a mean version of what anthropologists would look for in their paradise. But they are worth examining. Only our secular view of society prevents us from appreciating the ubiquitousness and strategy of their location and, in turn, their role in social organization.[3]

Goffman is arguing that the large-scale rituals of traditional societies — the great public, communal rites of birth, transition, vocation, and death which anthropologists and Christian liturgists so much admire — have been irretrievably lost in modern industrial cultures. What remains are tiny, almost microbial, rituals exchanged almost imperceptibly between private individuals. Translated into the language of Christian worship, Goffman's prediction means that large-scale community celebrations like baptism or Eucharist no longer possess the power to offer people a sense of the sacred. Instead, people search for that sense of the sacred in the smaller, more intimate world of personal relationships, private prayer and reflection, and interior self-examination.

Quite frankly, I find Goffman's predictions about the future of community rituals repulsive; at the same time, I think he has identified something important. What Goffman identifies as the inability of large-scale public rituals to mediate a sense of the sacred to people living in modern industrial cultures is reinforced by Christopher Lasch's recent assessment of American life, a life he identifies as lived in *The Culture of Narcissism*.[4] Lasch argues that Americans have lost both faith and interest in

3. Erving Goffman, *Relations in Public* (New York: Harper & Row, 1971) 63.
4. Christopher Lasch, *The Culture of Narcissism: American Life in an Age of Diminishing Expectations* (New York: W. W. Norton & Co., 1978).

the larger structures of public life and social responsibility. Increasingly, Americans are turning their attention, not *outward* toward social issues that demand political action, but *inward* toward the self. In a culture that is apparently breaking down socially and economically, our attention is riveted on strategies of self-survival, on what Lasch calls "the pernicious cult of intimacy." The high priests of our culture are not people who work for civil rights or social justice or the liberation of minority groups, but the therapists who can offer self-help, self-improvement, self-actualization, self-awareness, self-realization, self-fulfillment and self-esteem. Attention to social reality has been replaced by transcendental self-attention. The great American heroine is not Dorothy Day, with her *Loaves and Fishes,* but Gail Sheehy, with her *Passages* and predictable crises. We interpret adult life, not as a commitment to social responsibility in the public arena, but as a series of *internal* crises: the identity crisis of adolescence, the intimacy crisis of young adulthood, the midlife crisis, and the crisis of aging. What commands our fascinated attention is the survival of the self through the crises ranging from intimacy to aging.

All these things—the collapse of communal rituals, the culture of narcissism, the inexhaustible preoccupation with self-survival—have affected our ability to sense the sacred in the rites and symbols of public worship. The conclusion is inescapable: increasingly, we identify our deepest religious experiences (our most profound sense of the sacred), not with public ritual and worship, but with private, personal experiences of intimacy and relationship. To put it another way, our primary model for the sacred (otherwise known as "the holy" or "the numinous") is *intimacy, not liturgy.* The "age of anxiety," ushered in with nuclear brilliance at Hiroshima in 1945, has yielded to the "age of intimacy," the "age of sharing and caring," the "age of the meaningful relationship." We look for the holy to reveal itself, not in the awe-inspiring rites of baptism and Eucharist, but in the awesome precincts of the self.

This, perhaps, is the most difficult problem we face today as liturgists. It is not that our reformed liturgy has destroyed the sense of the sacred or that the English vernacular has robbed the rite of its mystery. Such is the argument of James Hitchcock,[5] but I consider him to be entirely mistaken. Hitchcock contends that, if we could retrieve the old Latin ritual (the "Tridentine Mass"), we would recover our vanishing sense of the sacred. This is an utterly simplistic solution to a problem which, at root, is not liturgical at all, but cultural and sociological. The problem is not that the Latin liturgy was an adequate vehicle for communicating the sacred, while the revised rites are not; the problem is that with the rise and development of modern industrial cultures our sense of the sacred has shifted location. The sacred is no longer situated "outside," in the large, public celebrations of a community; it is located "inside," in the personal history and geography of the self.

An example may serve to illustrate this shift of sensibility. A few years ago Annie Dillard, a young American writer, wrote an astonishing book called *Pilgrim at Tinker Creek*, a journal of her experience as a solitary living beside a small creek in Virginia. Annie Dillard is a Christian, and her book frequently appeals to symbols derived from the Bible and Christian tradition. There is one particularly exquisite passage in the book where she describes an experience of intense contemplative insight:

> One day I was walking along Tinker Creek thinking of nothing at all and I saw the tree with the lights in it. I saw the backyard cedar where the mourning doves roost charged and transfigured, each cell buzzing with flame. I stood on the grass with the lights in it, grass that was wholly fire, utterly focused and utterly dreamed. It was less like seeing than like being for the first time seen, knocked breathless by a powerful glance. The flood of fire abated, but I'm still spending the power. Gradually the lights went out in the

---

5. James Hitchcock, *The Recovery of the Sacred* (New York: Seabury Press, 1974).

cedar, the colors died, the cells unflamed and disappeared. I was still ringing. I had been my whole life a bell, and never knew it until at that moment I was lifted and struck. I have since only very rarely seen the tree with the lights in it. The vision comes and goes, mostly goes, but I live for it, for the moment when the mountains open and a new light roars in spate through the crack, and the mountains slam.[6]

These words are hauntingly beautiful, and they clearly reveal a woman whose sense of the sacred is extraordinary. But close attention to this passage, to the description of "the tree with the lights in it," reveals that the experience is intensely personal and private. The word "I" appears ten times in this short passage; there are no references to "we" or "us." Indeed, the experience is unrelated to any other human companions. Unlike the gospel account of Jesus' transfiguration, for instance, there is no human community present to share or continue the vision. This is a "peak experience" centered upon a single individual, a solitary.

I am not trying to suggest that Annie Dillard's experience was imperfect, illegitimate, or selfish. Quite obviously, it was an experience of dramatic consequence for her vision of life and of the sacred. I am simply pointing out that the sense of the sacred in Dillard's description of the tree with lights in it is centered on the intimate interior relation between self and other: "I was still ringing. I had been my whole life a bell, . . . I was lifted and struck." This is a peak experience of the sacred that needs no community, no companions, no ritual, no liturgy. It is an experience which many of us find extremely attractive.

The point being made here is not that Annie Dillard is antiliturgical or that mystics and contemplatives are self-centered, but simply that for many Christians, the model for experiencing the sacred is one derived from direct immediate personal experience, rather than one derived from the rites and symbols of a

---

6. Annie Dillard, *Pilgrim at Tinker Creek* (New York: Harper Magazine Press, 1974) 33-34.

people's liturgy. We expect our "peak experiences" to happen, not at a parish liturgy on Sunday morning, but at moments of deep personal sharing (in marriage, for instance) or at private times of centering prayer, private meditation, and contemplative communion with nature.

There is a growing discrepancy, in other words, between what the liturgy traditionally claims to do — namely, mediate the sacred — and what many of us are looking for in a religious experience. In summary, our problem is not that we have lost our sense of the sacred, but that we no longer expect the liturgy to be the primary locus for such experience. Our central — if often unconscious — symbol of the sacred is not the community at public prayer, but the solitary pilgrim at Tinker Creek. Our primary — though, again, often unconscious — symbol of religious experience is not Jesus' transfiguration among a community of apostles and prophets, but self-transformation through a personal vision of the "tree with the lights in it."

II. The Problem: Its Origins and Causes

The suggestion, then, is that our sense of the sacred has moved, shifted its location; that the sacred has become disengaged from its earlier location among a community of people at public prayer. It is further suggested that many of the reasons for this relocation are embedded in cultural and sociological factors, particularly in what Nicholas Lasch describes as the "culture of narcissism" — the preoccupation with self-survival and intimacy, as opposed to social concern and generativity. But it must also be admitted that some of the trouble we experience in relating our sense of the sacred to the celebration of liturgy has been caused by the process of liturgical reform itself, in particular by two of its characteristics: professionalism and authoritarianism.

Professionalism. At the time of Vatican II, the Church attempted something entirely unprecedented in Christian history: a complete reform of its public worship by engaging the services of historians, liturgical specialists, and theological experts. In some respects, of course, this "reform by the experts" was inevitable, welcome, and necessary. The context was, after all, that of an international community with a strong centralized government and a ritual tradition which had been frozen for nearly four hundred years. The work of historians and professional liturgists was essential if the reform were to reflect the important developments of theology and the social sciences which had occurred since the Council of Trent in the sixteenth century.

Nevertheless, professionals have their limitations: they tend to think that all problems can be solved, given sufficient quantities of time, catechesis, and instruction. The difficulty with this approach, however, is that popular religious rituals are not born in libraries or classrooms, but rather tend to develop in fits and starts as a community slowly accumulates a tradition, develops a pattern of experience, and reflects on its history. The most popular and enduring religious rituals are those which speak directly to common experience: to being born, getting married, planting crops, gathering food, growing sick, and dying. These are ritual events which touch upon the most ordinary and indispensable human needs. That is why popular religious rites are often messy, exotic, erotic, and even theologically suspect. One thinks of the Italian neighborhood that celebrates St. Anthony of Padua with processions through the streets and a statue plastered with dollar bills or of the phallic candle and watery womb of the Paschal Vigil. These liturgical and not-so-liturgical rites reflect basic human needs — social, sexual, economic — yet none of these rites was created by a team of professional experts.

This is not to denigrate the work of liturgical scholars, but simply to indicate the limitations of what they can do in reforming popular rites. While the liturgy cannot obviously be subject to popular referendum each Sunday, one cannot but wonder whether the "new liturgy" might not have looked rather different if the first step of the reform had been made from the ground up, rather than from the top down.

Authoritarianism. Related to this issue of reform by professionals is what can only be called "liturgical authoritarianism." For more than a thousand years, Christians have been estranged from the language of the liturgy, ever since Latin ceased to be the language of the common folk and became the specialized language of the "upper crust": clergy and monks, lawyers and merchants, nobles and diplomats. Many European vernaculars were already well developed by the middle of the ninth century — Old French, for example — and had become the language of everyday speech for the majority of Christian people. The failure to adopt the language of the people meant, in effect, that liturgical power (like other forms of power) was effectively withheld from the people, for whoever controls the official language owns the power. Language is, in fact, the fundamental form of human power; loss of language thus means loss of power. Notice, then, that the estrangement of the people from Latin language and Latin liturgy was as much a political and social fact as it was a religious and liturgical one. Latin belonged to the clergy, and so did the liturgy.

By reintroducing vernacular languages into worship, the Second Vatican Council was taking a step in the direction of restoring power to the people. The problem is, however, that after giving the language back to the people, reenfranchising them linguistically, there has been a consistent refusal to give them any real power of decision-making. To put it very bluntly, the Roman Church is still a Church dominated by the power of ordained celibate men. The people have been given the right to use their own language, but they are still forbidden to speak. It is true that there are increasing numbers of lay people active in ministries at the local and even the diocesan level; it is true that there are parish councils and diocesan commissions. But when the big decisions are made — about marriage, family, sexuality, pastoral leadership, community prayer, and worship — the people are suddenly disenfranchised; they lose the vote. About a hundred years ago, the controversial yet farsighted Catholic theologian John Baptist Hirscher made some comments which caused his works to be put on the Index of Forbidden Books. Nevertheless, they ring very true today:

> Where there is no participation, there can be no interest. . . . No one interests himself in a matter in which he can take no real part. . . . The people in our day are submissive only to such ordinances and regulations as they themselves have had a share in establishing, and of which the utility and the reason are perceptible.[7]

Hirscher went on to propose that every diocese should have a synod in which lay Christians were a direct part of the policy- and decision-making process, and he warned against packing such a synod with people whose views simply echoed the bishop's own.

The important point here is that Hirscher recognized the important link between participation and interest: "participation" includes not only liturgical participation (Hirscher had already called for the use of the vernacular in the 1830s), but participation at the level of decision and policy. Perhaps this helps to explain why, even after our liturgical reforms, a sense of frustration, discontent, and disaffection has continued to grow in the Church. We have tried to give language without power, participation in liturgy without correlative participation at the level of decision and policy.

Under these conditions, we should not be surprised if the liturgy fails to mediate a "sense of the sacred." To experience the sacred is, after all, to experience power: power generated and released, power that empowers, power that shapes a vision and discloses responsibilities. If, however, we deny people any direct role in shaping that vision and assuming that responsibility, then we effectively deny them any sense of the sacred. Perhaps that is one reason why so many Christians are seeking the sacred

---

7. John Baptist Hirscher, *Sympathies of the Continent, or Proposals for a New Reformation*, trans. A. C. Coxe (Oxford: John Henry Palmer, 1852) 131, 149.

elsewhere: in a charismatic community or prayer meeting; in the cult of intimacy and relationships; in the private precincts of centering prayer and meditation; in the religious traditions of the East — Buddhist, Hindu, Islamic.

In summary, liturgical authoritarianism has given the people the power of participation in language without giving them significant power of participation in church policy, decision-making, ministry, and mission. That is why many believe that recent documents such as *Inaestimabile donum* are not really concerned with liturgy at all, but with power. These are basically political documents aimed at preserving a structure of authority which consistently refuses to enfranchise the people fully in matters of doctrine, worship, morality, and mission.

III. What Can Be Done?

The thrust of the argument so far has been quite straightforward: liturgy will continue to have trouble mediating a sense of the sacred to people as long as people feel that they are not being listened to on vital matters of belief, behavior, liturgy, and mission. The tactic so far has been to give people back their language while denying them the power of responsibility, and it just is not working. For many, the liturgy continues to be boring and insipid, not because it is in English, or because it has been revised, or because it is celebrated facing them, or because it uses bread that looks and tastes like bread. It is boring and insipid because people are being duped into accepting responsibility without power, ministry without recognition, participation without decision-making, and change without the franchise. The sacred, of its nature, empowers; the sacred raises up and enables. But the liturgy seems to empower no one with anything, except those already in power; it merely invites the participants to return next week and try it again. How, then, can we restore a sense of the sacred to our liturgies?

Sense of the Sacred

First, we have to cease treating the liturgy as though it were some benign form of religious manipulation or crowd control. Presiders must begin to act more like worshipers and less like proprietors of a place of entertainment. Their motto has been given to them by Robert Hovda: strong, loving, and wise.[8] The president of the assembly is simply a Christian worshiper who is strong enough to withstand the onslaught of God's awesome and demanding presence; loving enough to bless the dirt under an old man's fingernail; and wise enough to know the difference between the two.

Second, we have to become far more discriminating about the decisive impact which secular culture has on Christians. The "culture of narcissism" is not an invention of Christopher Lasch; the cult of self-help, self-awareness, self-actualization, self-growth, and intimacy *is* pernicious. Curiously enough, this kind of narcissistic attention to self appears rather dominant in contemporary instances of Christian spirituality. A recent survey of attitudes towards prayer among students and priest-alumni of a large midwestern seminary reveals that the student population in particular sees prayer as a kind of self-analysis that affords opportunity for growth in self-awareness and intimate relationships.[9] Personal prayer was characterized as "nostalgia, reflected regret, New Year's resolutions, or an examination of conscience."[10] Liturgical prayer, which appears to play an ever diminishing role in the spirituality of seminary students, was seen primarily as "private prayer in a communal setting."[11] Attitudes like these reveal the profound impact of a narcissistic culture—"transcendental self-attention"—on many young people today, particularly upon those who offer themselves as can-

---

8. Robert Hovda, *Strong, Loving and Wise—Presiding in Liturgy* (Washington: The Liturgical Conference, 1976).
9. *Learning to Pray Alone*, ed. D. Buchlein and K. Stasiak (St. Meinrad, Ind.: St. Meinrad School of Theology, 1980) 21-22.
10. *Ibid.* 23.
11. *Ibid.* 96.

didates for ordained ministry. If these are the attitudes shaping the piety of the Church's inevitable future leadership, then, to say the very least, there remains much to be desired, much to be worked for.

Third, the people must have a much more active and decisive role in shaping the practical policies of worship and mission in the Church. We cannot continue to ask people to participate actively in the Church's worship if we continue to deny them a voice in matters of belief and behavior. As John Baptist Hirscher said, "Where there is no participation there can be no inerest. . . . No one interests himself in a matter in which he can take no real part."

If the liturgy, then, is to be—or to become—a primary source of the sense of the sacred among our people, we are going to have to face, and to resist, the strong cultural inclination to identify the sacred with the self, the holy with the intimate, the divine with the private and personal. Liturgy is, after all, a calling forth, a summons to mission, a challenge to move beyond where we are now to a future that is God. At its deepest root, Christian liturgy is *parable*—a provocative assault on our customary way of viewing life, world, and others. It is in the midst of that discomfiting liturgical provocation that we meet the sacred, the Holy One whose face is simultaneously human and not human, strange and familiar, attractive and repelling. This is the God that worship seeks to reveal; this is the God that Christians claim to encounter in Jesus Christ.

Liturgical Creativity

LOUIS WEIL

Anglican apologetics for liturgy, going back to the seventeenth and eighteenth centuries, talked a great deal about the beauty of holiness in the Anglican liturgy and expressed a concern with dignity and esthetic quality in regard to architecture and setting. To this day, the English have a remarkable ability when it comes to staging a procession. Although no one can do a procession quite like the British, Anglicans are hardly thought of as being creative. A friend of mine was traveling around England a few years ago, and, while visiting a churchyard, he found the grave of an Anglican priest of the eighteenth century. The tombstone read: "Here lies the Reverend John Smith, who preached in the pulpit of this church for thirty years without enthusiasm."[1]

It was the result of what I would call a typical Anglican conservatism that the creativity, as it was labeled, of about a decade or so ago was looked on generally in the Episcopal Church with some hesitancy. There is no question, of course, that creative experiments in the liturgy were going on in the Episcopal Church,

---

1. "Enthusiasm" was a common reference to the Methodist movement and its excesses (from an Anglican point of view) during that century.

LOUIS WEIL, a priest of the Episcopal Church, is past president of the North American Academy of Liturgy. He received his S.T.D. from the Catholic Institute of Paris, served for ten years as a missionary in Latin America, and is currently professor of liturgics and church music at Nashotah House, an Episcopal seminary in Wisconsin.

just as among Roman Catholics. We saw practices that were new or unusual, but with them a tentativeness, or a loss of reference to the traditional context. As a result, there was inevitably some hesitancy in embracing the cause of liturgical creativity. For many people in the Episcopal Church, what they experienced was a kind of chaotic unfamiliarity. I believe, as we look back on that decade of activity, that we were seeing a kind of pendulum swing. The liturgical traditions had been so rigid for so long that, inevitably, when we began to try new practices, the pendulum went all the way in the other direction.

We are at a point now of making a synthesis of great importance. This frightens people because of a kind of marriage to the printed text. I remember a priest, some twenty years ago, who became very upset over the removal of an asterisk from the official Prayer Book version of the *Nunc Dimittis*. The asterisk came at a very awkward place: "For mine eyes have seen * thy salvation." The director of music at my seminary had removed the asterisk for the musical flow of the phrase. The visiting alumnus commented, "Once you change one asterisk, it's all up for grabs." In a sense, he was right; because once one allows that the printed page is not an absolute, is not something which demands total conformity, then, in fact, one opens the door to a very different approach to the liturgy. What happens is that liturgical innovation inevitably shatters a rigidified *status quo*. I think that this had to take place for the Church once again to come to what liturgical prayer is called to be.

A lot of the problems of a decade ago can be easily caricatured, but what do we do with the question of creativity today? Are we at a time for synthesis between tradition and innovation? Little of the earlier innovation has lasted. I see in the Episcopal Church, at least, a kind of retrenchment. Now that we have a revised prayer book, a new kind of rigidity is already setting in. A year ago, some of my students at Nashotah House, in an evening of spoofing at the faculty, did a caricature of me in which in the year 2010, from my deathbed, I was a defender of the Book of Common Prayer of 1979. I hope I shall avoid falling into the trap that so many of my fellow Episcopalians fell into with the previous 1928 prayer book. We now have new rites. But more important, a new mentality must go with them. That cuts across the board. It applies to all the liturgical churches. But what I see happening is the reassertion of the old rubrical mentality which wants to tie down all the pieces to a cautiously familiar model and to be sure that all the pieces are intact. I have heard priests say, "Now that we have the new liturgy, just tell me how to do it, and I'll do it the way I'm supposed to." But this is the same mentality: "Give me a fixed norm." This obliges us to dig much more deeply into the question of creativity. What is the character of creativity, *authentic* creativity, not just a polarized innovation that is trying to get away from rigid rubricism? What is the authentic character of creativity? What is its abiding place in liturgical development, its pastoral significance, and its dynamic? How does creativity work?

The question of creativity in the liturgy poses itself with special vigor because we seem to be living in a time when the classical model—let's say, the shape of the Roman liturgy— which was established by the time of Pope Gregory the Great (and even in its later forms in the missal of Pius V), is giving way or breaking. The work of Vatican II was to restore the classical model to its integrity. In fact, once that work was done, once the classical models were restored, we found ourselves at the edge of an abyss. We live in radically different cultural and social situations with a whole new pattern of pastoral imperatives. Band-Aids on the classical model don't seem to suffice anymore. A new vision and a new breath are going to be a necessity for the living celebration of those rites. In this context, creativity is an imperative for survival. I believe we are at the end of the classical model. Creative innovation will certainly modify the model significantly and, possibly, will shatter it.

It is difficult to anticipate what new model will emerge. I believe the firmest basis would be a model drawn from the

Church, the concept of the liturgy as the worship of a gathered people. Although we cannot design a blueprint, certain insights are available, especially if we can learn from the history of the liturgy how the maturing of the classical model led to the discouragement of creativity. Sensitive criticism in this regard can offer a real contribution to creative development in the future. We should look at what has happened in the evolution of the classical model for insight into where we need to move and where, in fact, creativity can make a significant contribution.

One of the signs of the maturity of the classical model of the Roman Rite was its concern with what one might call craftsmanship. The high quality of the classical rites as vehicles of corporate prayer was achieved through a kind of polishing effect of centuries of organic experience within the prayer life of a church. The prayers of the tradition had been prayed for a very long time and had become the vehicle of prayer for people in widely differing circumstances. The prayers were like polished stones, and the beauty of the classical forms was shaped by their use in liturgical prayer in such diverse situations. They have a quality which spontaneous prayer, however inspired it may be in a certain context, simply does not have. Once those classical forms had crystallized, attention shifted from the *meaning* of corporate prayer to *how* the liturgy was done; in other words, the age of rubricism had arrived — the time when rubrics became an end in themselves, the attitude of doing the liturgy according to the rules. The Church developed a preoccupation with method or technique. Form became more important than spirit, and the means triumphed over the ends.

The purpose of the classical liturgy, certainly in its origin, was to be a vehicle of corporate prayer. The very perfection of the classical model then became a suffocating force upon the purpose for which it existed, so that spiritual energy was poured more into the performance of the approved form and custom than into *being the Church at prayer*, which, after all, is the central meaning of corporate worship.

I. Tradition versus Creativity

Our point of departure for a discussion of the relation of tradition to creativity is drawn from Jewish liturgical study. It offers insight into what may be an inevitable process in any liturgical evolution, and certainly the parallels between Jewish and Christian developments are illuminating. The rabbis during the period of the rabbinic commentaries (the early centuries of the Christian era) speak of prayer in terms of *kavvanah* and *keva*.[2] *Kavvanah* is spontaneous prayer — inward, pure, devout, concentrated, and free. *Kavvanah* is the necessary characteristic of true prayer. *Keva*, on the other hand, is traditional prayer. It is the prayer of routine. It gives continuity to the liturgical tradition. It is what makes the prayer recognizable as Jewish prayer. We all recognize this dynamic from experience: we find our identity as a Roman Catholic or an Episcopalian or a Lutheran in a certain continuity of form in the tradition. That, for the Jew, is *keva*, that is, the tradition. For the rabbis, *kavvanah* is the essential form of prayer, the prayer of the heart. Without that authentic prayer, formal prayer, *keva*, is but a lifeless shell. For this reason, the rabbis were generally opposed to the writing down of prayer. There was no written order of service until the ninth century of the Christian era. In other words, the oral tradition of the liturgy continued to be normative in Judaism long after Christianity had begun to codify its rites in written manuscripts. In Judaism, the oral tradition of the liturgy continued until well into the Middle Ages, by which time Christian liturgical manuscripts were already undergoing significant development.

What is fascinating about the *kavvanah-keva* distinction in Judaism is that one generation's *kavvanah* becomes another generation's *keva*. That is, the spontaneous, free prayer which

2. For a discussion of *kavvanah* and *keva* in Jewish sources, see Louis Jacobs, *Hasidic Prayer* (New York: Schocken Books, 1973) 70-92 *passim*, and Jakob J. Petuchowski, *Understanding Jewish Prayer* (New York: Ktav Publishing House, 1972) 3-25 *passim*.

sprang to the lips of inspired believers in one period became the fixed form or the tradition — the *keva* — of the next generation. Contemporary Jewish liturgical scholars acknowledge that this led to a kind of cumulative situation. Inspired *kavvanah* was eventually canonized as *keva*, so there was a constant accretion to the liturgy. Even when an element ceased to have any relevance, it was still prayed because it was part of the tradition. It had originated as spontaneous prayer in a given situation. It was canonized so that even when the situation changed, the tradition retained it. Orthodox Jews still pray for the leaders of the Babylonian Academies which have not existed for a thousand years, quite an example of the abiding quality of *keva*. At Nashotah House, a much hallowed prayer, a holy *keva*, which is used at the seminary twice a year, prays for all kings and princes, whereas, on all the other days of the year, we pray somewhat more realistically for the President and the Congress. This is a very traditional prayer which, on those two days, I have still not dared to touch — holy *keva*.

Jewish liturgists comment that the *kavvanah*-to-*keva* progression, that is, from spontaneity to tradition, inevitably leads to the triumph of *keva*: rigidity triumphs. The parallel to Christian liturgical history is strong. It helps us to understand why creativity is a problem. The truly inspired and effective spontaneous element is all too easily canonized. Most of us have taken part in a liturgy with new music or some other fresh element which we have then wanted to use ourselves in other situations. The element which is spontaneous and fresh in one situation easily becomes fixed, and something which is extremely appropriate on one occasion, where it is genuine, is taken into other occasions, where it really is not as appropriate. Eventually, published or rubricated, this spontaneous prayer or music becomes, then, in turn, part of the problem. It becomes part of the fixed and inflexible tradition. For example, scholars who have studied the history of the Roman Canon, Eucharistic Prayer I of the Roman Rite, note that certain sections of the prayer came as later developments of the prayer in association with specific celebrations and specific contexts. In due course, all those flexible or variable elements became fixed and rigidified. The advent of printing in the fifteenth century made that rigidity all the more precise, so that printing, combined with the tendency toward fixation, led to an unprecedented rigidification of the liturgy. It is fascinating also, for example, to look at the history of the Hail Mary, which in the eleventh and twelfth centuries had enormous flexibility. The evolution of this prayer shows it to have had a variety of forms. The same is true of the *Confiteor*, which had an enormous diversity, both in the religious orders and in local diocesan use. The form varied virtually from diocese to diocese. Eventually the pattern narrowed down, and, with the invention of printing, the absolute rigidification of the liturgical form was complete.[3] Thus, from the fifteenth century a level of inflexibility, previously unknown, was achieved.

It is little wonder that now, after five hundred years of this rigidification, we are trying to rediscover the authentic sources of liturgical creativity within the Christian experience. We are at the end of an extraordinary period of liturgical rigidity. The comment I have heard within the Episcopal Church is, "Why so much change so suddenly?" It is precisely because there has been so little organic, natural evolution for such an extraordinary period of time during which an enormous degree of social upheaval has taken place.

The rabbinic commentaries on *kavvanah*, spontaneity, and *keva*, tradition, always held out as an ideal that traditional prayer should be invested with the spirit of spontaneous prayer. It is a marvelous ideal, but not always realized. The rabbinic solution to this tension between tradition and spontaneity is exemplified in the history of what are known as the Eighteen Bene-

---

3. Herbert Thurston, *Familiar Prayers* (Westminster, Md.: Newman, 1953) 73–114.

dictions in the Jewish Liturgy, one of the fundamental elements of Jewish prayer. At first, the tradition was only that there were eighteen of them. Eventually, the subject of each benediction came to be fixed. But even within the determination of the subject, the Jews maintain a freedom of wording and even a flexibility of context. In other words, even within the fixed form, there was still space for the spontaneous element: in a prayer for God's gift of health, one was quite free to mention someone who was specifically ill. There was freedom within the fixed context. This balance gives us an important insight into the question of spontaneity versus fixity in Christian liturgical rites.

The reaction against creativity of a decade ago presumed an either/or situation—either one had a thoroughly creative spontaneous liturgical experience or one conformed to the rubrics. I am convinced that good liturgy is a fusion, a joining, a marriage of these two elements. Good liturgy is never random. It is formed around such fundamental symbols that a haphazard approach seems to trivialize, often in spite of good intentions, very fundamental aspects of Christian faith. I call it the threat of the giggle. Some liturgical experimentation, although well-intentioned, suggests that the act is as trivial as styrofoam cups of coffee. The vessel, the vehicle, says a great deal. One must not treat the forms too lightly. To say that, however, is in no way to deny the crucial importance of creativity. Creativity always takes place in a specific context. Creativity requires not only sound craftsmanship, a knowledge of the dynamics of the liturgy, but also a deep sensitivity to the pastoral reality. When students who have been out of seminary for a few years ask me for my opinion on a liturgical matter, it is difficult to give any kind of precise answer unless I have known the community in which they are serving. One must not divorce that kind of decision from the context of the specific human situation.

Good liturgy draws constantly upon the resources available from the tradition, that is, the forms which have been polished by generations of corporate prayer and which were once, in many cases, the spontaneous prayer of an earlier generation. But the tradition must always be newly and freshly invested with the spirit of spontaneous prayer, the creative prayer which springs from the reality of a given human situation. One cannot decide about those questions in the abstract. It is always a specific people at a specific place under specific circumstances. The rhythms of the tradition are not lost, but they are given new life in their creative celebration in a living context. The creation of liturgy for our own time and place does not oblige us to scorn the tradition nor to ignore the authorized liturgical books. But it does oblige us to expose those classical rhythms and forms so that they may take root as a living plant in the Church today and not remain merely an externalized form.

I am convinced that the fundamental elements of the tradition have that splendid and flexible universality which permit such constant adaptation and renewal. This may be seen in such a prayer as the Lord's Prayer, to use the most obvious example. It is a form which we have all prayed in an incredible variety of circumstances, yet the universality of the prayer manifests itself in joy and pain, in times of great difficulty and in times of normal everyday existence. It is because of this quality as authentic *keva* that this prayer has that universality. Our *keva*, the tradition that we have received, can surely bear the risk of transformation by *kavvanah*. If it cannot, that is perhaps the most serious judgment we can make upon it. What we need, then, is a perpetual dialogue, a synthesis between the tradition and the creative sources.

II. COUNTERCREATIVE ELEMENTS

In order to explore creativity, we must also discuss what is countercreative, for there are countercreative dynamics to be found in the history of the liturgy. As with Jewish prayer, the Christian liturgical *keva* resists the intrusion of anything new. Innovation, after all, is very threatening. It is unpredictable. It threatens to shatter our security, the security of what is familiar. As we have seen, it is precisely the maturity of the classical tradition, its concern with technique, style, or method, which discourages innovation. I would like to focus attention on three countercreative dynamics which are quite evident in the Church's liturgical tradition and certainly are with us still.

The first countercreative dynamic is *minimalism,* which is the tendency to reduce. It often manifests a preoccupation with validity. A friend once asked me, "Why on earth is it taking you two years to do the course work in liturgy? It doesn't take that long to learn the rubrics." He was not intending to be funny. The question of validity had been imposed upon his understanding of sacramental celebrations. Inevitably, then, liturgy simply involves learning the rules. This, of course, creates an approach primarily concerned with the use of the proper method to get the proper result. How much water poured for a baptism is absolutely necessary for it to be valid? How much bread must be used or how much wine or how many communicants in order to have a valid Mass? Such questions have been answered out of the life of the Church from what is an authentic pastoral concern with how to deal with an extreme situation. How does one deal with the possibility that a priest might find himself quite isolated in a given circumstance or that there might be only a very, very modest amount of bread and wine available? Obviously, the Church has to say, "Beyond this point, we don't recognize it as the act of the Church." But the problem is that this kind of answering to the special situation leads to a normalization of that model. There are many examples in liturgical history. The effect is a kind of minimalism in which we lose the common sense of the fundamental, normative signs. Baptism is a washing. Under all normal circumstances, one does not have to ask if a thimble of water is enough. Abundant water is usually available.

This is not just a Roman Catholic problem. I was godfather at a baptism several years ago at which a bishop was performing the rite. As we approached the baptismal font I saw, to my horror, that there was no water filling the font, but rather, in the middle of the font there was a beautiful shell filled with water. More terrible still, the bishop never picked up the shell, but simply dipped his fingers into it and allowed water to flow three times over the child's forehead. It could hardly have been less manifest that a washing was taking place. With Mass, too, the Eucharist as a gathering of God's people for what is a true eating and drinking must be evident in the action. Other expressions of minimalism can be found, for example, in the Missal of Pius V. In the missal used before Vatican II, the great processional psalms were reduced to snippits, to single verses. The diverse ministries of the classical rite from the period of Gregory the Great were reduced to the dominant ministry of a solitary priest; a single priest at the altar became the normative form. The marvelous physical and verbal participation of the laity in the classical rite was reduced to passive silence. Here again is a case where the reduction to what is possible at the minimal level becomes the normative model. Valid—yes, of course, valid— but the minimum. If we ask the wrong question, we are likely to get the wrong answer. The greater question, the more important question, one which encompasses the question of validity, is the question of sign. Certainly, what I have described is an impoverished expression of the meanings which the Eucharist is intended to bear.

The second countercreative element is *rubricism.* Creativity is often not very tidy. A polished traditionalism requires tidiness, often compulsive tidiness. Certainly, good pastoral norms and guidelines are needed for our liturgical celebrations, but not rigid rules which suppress a sound pastoral sense. I must not be obliged to set aside my own pastoral judgment to obey rules which I see to be counterproductive in terms of the gathered community.

Several years ago, some students talked me into celebrating the Sarum Rite of about the year 1530. This was the classical

Roman Rite as celebrated in England just prior to the Reformation. As we tried to plan the liturgy, we found ourselves in a tug-of-war with the building. The chapel at Nashotah House is not laid out in agreement with the rubrics of the Sarum Missal, which presumed a celebration in Salisbury Cathedral. The architectural layout underlying the rite was quite different in many fundamental ways from the layout of the chapel at Nashotah House. In the fifteenth and sixteenth centuries, when that rite was normative in much of England, good pastors must have made commonsense adaptations for other buildings. This gives us, I think, a perspective on the role of rubrics. To a great extent, the history of rubrics is the history of a local use gaining respect in the Church, through which means its norms are universalized or at least accepted over a wide area of the Church.

The same thing is true of many of the rubrics of the Roman Rite of the Missal of Pius V. Many of the rubrics presume the papal liturgies, presume even in some cases that Mass is being celebrated at the altar of St. Peter's Basilica. Such rubrics, if they are taken literally, inhibit the celebration of a rite in a different setting. These rubrics were canonized because a given church had gained importance within the Church as a place in which the liturgy had been celebrated with love, with care, with a sense of beauty. But we must distance ourselves from an excessive rigidity in approaching those rubrics. When we take them too literally, we fall into the countercreative problem of rubricism, where the rules become an end in themselves. Surely the post–Vatican II spirit is to see the rubrics as guidelines to be adapted to a real human situation with pastoral sensitivity. In this perspective, rubrics require the complement of at least normal creativity.[4]

4. Since this paper was delivered, an extensive treatment of criteria for the interpretation of liturgical law has been published; see John M. Huels, "The Interpretation of Liturgical Law," *Worship* 55, no. 3 (May 1981) 218-237. See also Thomas Richstatter, *Liturgical Law: New Style, New Spirit* (Chicago: Franciscan Herald Press, 1977) and R. Kevin Seasoltz, *New Liturgy, New Laws* (Collegeville, Minn.: The Liturgical Press, 1980).

Liturgical Creativity

The third countercreative element is *clericalism*. For many centuries, the liturgy has been seen as the domain of the hierarchy, and again, this is not a narrowly Roman Catholic problem. When I was a student in Paris, I was asked to take part in an ecumenical program during the Week of Prayer for Christian Unity. It was being held at a French Huguenot parish, and the entire liturgy had been planned by the pastor of the church. There were, of course, Roman Catholic, Anglican, Orthodox, and various Protestant clergy in the group, and also a wide representation of laity from all those traditions. To my amusement, but also my disappointment, we learned that every element in the liturgy, as predetermined by the Huguenot pastor, had been assigned to a member of the clergy.

Clericalism is not just a problem which pervades Christianity. Nor is it only the fault of the clergy. Many of the laity are content to be passive and to allow the clergy to control the Church's corporate prayer life. It takes them off the hook. The problem with having a clerically dominated liturgy (and I am not referring to appropriate liturgical leadership) is that it does not correspond to the diverse nature of the Body of Christ which is composed of many members.

The transition away from clericalism is very difficult. I once thought it would be easier than it has turned out to be. New patterns of parish worship, the involvement of the laity in the planning and celebration of the liturgy, are obviously an imperative and, at the same time, will be achieved only painfully and gradually. A necessary complement to this evolution is the need for new patterns of seminary education without which little is going to change. If hierarchical domination persists in the seminaries, where everything is predetermined without consultation of the members of that community, it is likely that most of the graduates will perpetuate that model after ordination. That is my observation in the Episcopal Church.

Minimalism, rubricism, and clericalism: these, it seems to me, pose the greatest threat to creativity in the worship of our parishes. In a real sense, the defining of those problems locally is a task which each one of us must do in terms of the particularities of our own situation. In my own experience, I have seen these three countercreative elements at work in a great variety of ways. They are subtle and insidious. They suffocate authentic creativity.

III. Beyond the Boundaries

The parish context, on Sunday in particular, places certain constraints upon the range of creativity for a variety of reasons. The Church is made up of many members, and the Sunday Eucharist encompasses a wide diversity among its people, including age, spirituality, and attitude. If the liturgy is to be an instrument of the unity of God's people, then the planners must be very sensitive to the levels of innovation which are incorporated into the Sunday liturgy. A considerable degree is possible, more than is generally undertaken; but the diversity of the gathering must be a serious pastoral concern.

I had a marvelous experience some two years ago. Within one week's time, I had the opportunity to see an innovation in a traditional parish situation complemented by a breaking of the boundaries in a specialized context. Both involved dance. In Colorado there is a Christian community for which dance has become part of their normal prayer life. They were invited to a quite conservative parish and were asked to dance at the Offertory. They took into account the reality of the situation. The dance was of appropriate length and very appropriately integrated into the typical structure of the worship of that parish. The result was that the people, for whom the idea of dance in the liturgy would have been negative (if not abhorrent), had an extremely positive experience because of the sensitivity shown by the group to the nature of the Sunday context.

The other occasion was a workshop which took place at Nashotah House. Carla DeSola, a well-known liturgical dancer from New York, visits us every two years. Our dance liturgies do not take place in the church building because it evokes a quite traditionalist style. For these special liturgies, we do not allow the verbal element to dominate, as is characteristic of our traditional liturgies. As little as can be said is said. Everything that can be expressed through gesture, through movement, is done that way. In other words, the style is quite distinct from any typical parish worship. For those who enter into that experience, which is a special experience, it is a breaking of the boundaries. The experience of the people who participate opens up a vision of the liturgy which is not primarily verbal. The whole person is involved. Through such special situations, we who plan liturgies can, with a sense of proportion, gain insight which will permit us to begin to expand within the realities of our situation.

I have also pushed beyond the parochial boundaries in my work with children and the liturgy during the past several years. My goal is not to give them a watered down adult liturgy. Students work with me in planning these liturgies with only modest reference to the official texts. We start from the other end. Our goal is to get beneath the verbal dimension of the liturgy into the substructure of what is going on in those liturgies. We emphasize the basic signs so that the children, through movement, touch, water, color, dance, and all the various means available, may enter into the underlying liturgical elements, the underlying dynamics. What is interesting to me is that in both the dance liturgies and in the children's liturgies, the structure is traditional. There is the structural element of gathering. There is the communication of the word, not necessarily through the spoken word, but perhaps the acted word. Finally, there is always the eucharistic breaking of the bread and sharing of the cup which, of course, involve the Eucharistic Prayer. The fundamental structure is quite traditional. In other words, beneath these "beyond-the-present-boundaries" liturgies, we have the tradition in an interplay with creative elements. This is still the exceptional possibility, but it is a possibility which opens up for those who share in it a wider vision from which new models may begin to emerge. In that perspective, for us who share in these celebrations now, they are a foretaste.

New Forms for Parish Ministry

REGIS DUFFY, O.F.M.

For many today, the experience of parish and ministry is not very different from the *modus vivendi* that Lucy offered to Linus in a famous *Peanuts* cartoon: "Let's look at it this way: You and I belong to the same family, we have the same relatives, the same blood; in other words, kid, we're stuck together." Often enough, people are just hanging on, hoping that something will happen; yet in many places the atmosphere suggests not so much a community of people ministering to one another as a crowd of people on a commercial flight thrown together by the sheer accident of all wanting to arrive eventually at the same place.

Reflecting on my own experience of parish life, I find my memory drawn to two very different kinds of parish community. The parish I grew up in was in Brooklyn and was served by seven priests and a bishop who was the pastor. Back then, in the thirties and forties, we all thought it an extraordinarily fine parish: everyone agreed that we had good priests in abundance, and not many parishes were as fortunate. They served us well. But there is a difference between that parish of my youth and the

---

REGIS DUFFY is associate professor at the Washington Theological Union and has been a visiting professor at Princeton Theological Seminary. He holds a doctorate in sacramental theology from the Institut Catholique in Paris and has done postdoctoral work at the Sorbonne and the University of Würzburg. He served for three years on the pastoral team at the experimental parish of St. Séverin, Paris.

parishes I work in today: not only do the priests minister to the people, but the people in turn minister to the ministers, whoever they might be.

My own experience of a truly extraordinary parish, however, began when I became part of the team ministry at St. Séverin in Paris. This was the parish where team ministry actually originated, back in the 1940s. Even in those days, St. Séverin had things which have only recently been introduced into many parishes: the sacraments in the vernacular, Mass facing the people, face-to-face confessions. St. Séverin introduced a concept of team ministry, a team which included not only the priests, but people from the community. Even with all these innovations, however, I am convinced that that parish managed to stay alive only because they learned to play the game of musical chairs.

I have used the image of playing musical chairs before, but I want to use it again in this paper to illustrate what I mean when I talk about the "catechumenate model" for parish and go on to show that the catechumenate is more than simply a process for initiating Christians. Initiating Christians is really a second step, for it supposes a community into which people can be initiated. The first thing the catechumenate does, I maintain, is to teach people how to minister to one another. Without ministry there can be no initiation.

But I am not advancing this as mere theory. The catechumenate had been in practice for thirty years at St. Séverin by the time I arrived upon the scene and it had proved very successful. Its success lay, first, in teaching people who thought they were already Christians how to minister to one another and, only secondarily, in its ability to initiate non-Christians. Moreover, for at least three months out of every year, I continue to work in a team ministry in this country, and there I see the same model being successful in the same way. We are not just ten or fifteen men and women serving a parish; what is happening is that the talent for ministry is constantly being uncovered in people from whom it had never been evoked before. And so it happens that people who had hitherto regarded themselves as simply thrown together on the same flight have become people who have learned to recognize their ability, regardless of their age, to minister to one another.

People's experiences, of course, are different. Previous pastoral experiences may arouse a certain cynicism when confronted with this approach to ministry. It is important for each of us to look carefully at our experiences of parish life and to ask which parochial communities called us to engage in ministry and which ones simply frustrated us. Perhaps there have been parishes in our past which, when we thought we knew what our ministry was, called us to new and unexpected forms of service. Perhaps there have even been parishes where we found people who could help us discern what our ministerial gifts really were and so steered us in the right direction. Inevitably, this paper is the fruit of my own past experiences and, as such, cannot provide a blueprint for everyone else. Let it then serve as an invitation to others to recall their own autobiographical experiences of parish and parish ministry and therewith to confront the questions I will raise.

In this paper I will propose two things: first, that all ministries are forms of commitment to service; and, second, that commitment to service has always to be described, not in the abstract, but in terms of the stage that the would-be minister has reached in life and in terms of the needs of the community. It is quite different, for example, to offer oneself for ministry at the age of forty than at fifty-five. To ignore that fact is to run the risk of misdirecting people or of overlooking the possibility of new kinds of ministry. Moreover, there is no such thing as "community." There is the community of X and the community of Y. Community in the abstract does not exist. For this reason, it is quite misleading to use some general paradigm when we talk about ministries, for what is sufficiently general to fit everyone will not really fit anyone.

To avoid becoming impaled upon these dilemmas, I want to adopt a three-pronged approach. First, I will offer a *historical model* based upon the development of ministries in the apostolic and subapostolic churches. The facts are familiar enough, but it will be useful to review them in order to appreciate how much freedom the Church enjoys for the development, both in theology and in pastoral practice, of new forms of ministry. Second, I will describe the *catechumenal model* of ministry which developed out of what I shall describe as the historical model. Even in the second century, it was a startlingly new and creative development in response to needs arising in the community which no one had previously anticipated. Finally, I shall draw some tentative conclusions and open up some questions for our ongoing reflection.

I. The Historical Model

It is useful to begin by looking at the historical model if only because the impression is often given that the Church's ministry is forever and immutably restricted to the tripartite structure of bishop, priest, and deacon. Theologically that is not true, nor is it true historically. This is not to deny, of course, that the eventual development of the threefold ranking of episcopacy, presbyterate, and diaconate was legitimate, but simply to propose that it was not always thus, nor need it always be so restricted. No historian today would claim that these three orders existed, as they have come to us, from the beginning. This, in turn, suggests that the Church has the freedom to develop ministries which are appropriate for meeting the needs of its mission.[1] Lacking any blueprint for ministry, the churches of the apostolic and subapostolic period shaped their ministries in response to

---

1. My position does not differ radically from Karl Rahner's later thought on the subject; see his *Vorfragen zu einem ökumenischen Amtsverständnis* (Freiburg: Herder, 1974), especially pp. 70–76; see also the important article of E. Schillebeeckx, "The Christian Community and its Office Bearers," *Right of the Community to a Priest*, Concilium 133, ed. E. Schillebeeckx and J. Metz (New York: Seabury Press, 1980) 95–133.

New Forms of Ministry

two basic needs: continuity and flexibility. These two needs are always with us and will continue to shape the ministries of the Church, today and in the future.

Imagine the problems of trying to minister — either as a traveling missionary or as a member of a local community — in the period of the apostolic Church, around the year 75 A.D., for instance. What would our problem be as ministers of the gospel in Corinth or Rome or Ephesus, or even back in Jerusalem? I suggest that we would be challenged by the community about our claim to represent the Risen Lord. By what right could we claim that, by doing what we are doing, we are ministering to them as the Risen Lord ministered to those broken, suffering people — the disciples he encountered in the resurrection narratives? We would not be able to appeal to our seminary training, our ordination certificate, our master's degree in theology, as we can today.

Even today, however, that remains the challenge that people pose to us: What is our connection with the Risen Lord? Many today find our ministries unbelievable because they see no signs of the Lord. The credibility gap results from the fact that, on the one hand, there can be no ministry in Christ's name without him, but that, on the other hand, our being in continuity with him is not obvious. The same problem arose in the early Church, and Luke gives us an instance of how the problem was met. In Acts 2, Peter lists the qualifications required in one who is to fill the ministerial position vacated by Judas: such a person had to have eaten and drunk with the Lord during his earthly lifetime.

But, if this is what is required, how could Paul ever qualify as a minister of the Lord? Notice that Luke, with one exception, never speaks of Paul as an apostle, although Paul speaks of himself that way. The reason why Luke cannot call him an apostle is precisely that Paul's continuity with Jesus is problematic. To this objection, Paul responds with a new and startling argument which would undoubtedly have failed to convince Rome in later times: he claims to have seen the Lord. He was referring, of course, to his own conversion experience — an argument which any legalist would feel compelled to discount as irrelevant. Paul had to argue along these lines precisely because his opponents were telling the Corinthians that Paul, who established their church, was not an apostle. Paul cites his conversion experience of "seeing the Lord" to justify his ministry.[2]

This is a far cry from the model of ministry which developed in the early Middle Ages (and which has been very well described by Fr. Edward Kilmartin, S.J.).[3] In the medieval model, the minister came to be seen as someone who acted *in persona Christi* — a concept, incidentally, which the Eastern churches never accepted. This is a considerable change of perspective. To claim to act "in the person of Christ" is quite a different thing from claiming that one has a connection with the Risen Lord. The idea of acting "in the person of" someone is a concept borrowed from civil government. It was a very serviceable concept whose purpose was to safeguard the validity of administrative acts undertaken by alternates in the absence of the proper authority. Taken over by the Church, it was used to argue that when the unworthiness of the minister cast doubt on his connection with the Lord — that is, he was a bad minister — his sacramental action was still valid because he was acting only *in persona Christi*. Consequently, we may say that the principle of acting *in persona Christi* constituted a juridical-theological attempt to assure continuity when the credibility of ministry was being questioned.

But what did continuity with Christ mean in the early Church? The early Church saw the minister of Christ above all as a carrier of symbolic value. Ministry itself served as a symbol of the Risen Lord. Consequently, the most important credential

---

2. S. Freyne, *The Twelve: Disciples and Apostles* (London: Sheed and Ward, 1968) 247–54.

3. "Apostolic Office: Sacrament of Christ," *Theological Studies* 36 (1975) 243–64.

of a minister was his ability to symbolize for others precisely what the Risen Lord had done for his disciples on the lakeshore: reconcile disappointing followers. The strongest argument for the resurrection is not the empty tomb, but the way the flawed disciples became reconciled with the Crucified. After three years of traveling with Jesus, their discipleship was not completed. They learned how to be his ministers only because of his ministry to them after his resurrection from the dead. In the apostolic Church, then, continuity with Christ was the first requirement for ministry. That continuity consisted not in a juridical fiction, however — a matter of being invested with certain powers to do what other people could not do — but in a matter of fact, namely, the ability to operate effectively as a symbol of the Risen Lord.

The second requirement of the early Church was flexibility. There were two types of ministry in this period — local ministry based in a community and a wandering missionary ministry. The tensions between the two could become very acute, even in apostolic times. In Matthew's Gospel, for example, we find a number of references to "false prophets." Such references, even when placed upon the lips of Jesus, represent less his actual words than contemporary conflicts familiar to the evangelist. Prophets were usually traveling missioners, journeying from place to place. The warning against wolves in sheep's clothing is a warning against unworthy ministers claiming to be prophets (Matt 7:15-16).[4]

Another conflict occurred between the Jerusalem church and the gentile communities which were springing up and retaining many characteristics of their non-Jewish culture. At Jerusalem, the community was composed predominantly of converts from Judaism who, on becoming Christians, continued to think and act as Jews. One example of this continuity with their Jewish

---

4. See *Le Ministère et les ministères selon le Nouveau Testament*, ed. J. Delorme (Paris: Editions du Seuil, 1974) 202-204.

past was the model of community ministry — that of the synagogue — that they brought with them into Christianity.

Paul, as a Jewish convert, was quite familiar with the synagogue model, but in Corinth and Ephesus he was faced with a community of converts from paganism. Consequently, Paul developed structures which were so startlingly new to the people at Jerusalem that they grew alarmed and summoned him to Jerusalem to explain himself. But even within those two models, there was considerable flexibility. The Jerusalem model of a community council did not simply adopt the synagogue structure, but reshaped it to meet its own needs. Similarly, the New Testament mentions various "households of faith" in the gentile communities. These appear to have been families which served, in the first stage of the development of a local church, as headquarters for the area ministry: families such as those of Stephanus, Priscilla, etc.

In the period up to about 75 A.D., then, there appears to have been considerable flexibility in the development of ministries. Various developments, however, occurred in the next fifty years. First there was the problem of continuity: How could the Church be apostolic once all the apostles were dead? The problem hardly bothers us today because we rely on theories of apostolic succession as elaborated by the Scholastics or updated by Rahner. These theories, however, were not available in the first century, when the question continued to be posed in terms of a minister's connection with the Risen Lord. Now, however, the problem was one generation further removed. We notice an attempt to deal with this problem by a very clever change in terminology, found in the later New Testament writings.

The terms for minister in the first generation are expanded by the addition of new terms for second-generation ministries.[5] For example, in Pauline writings there is the famous saying which

---

5. See F. Schnider and W. Stenger, "The Church as a Building and the Building up of the Church," *Office and Ministry in the Church,* Concilium 80, ed. R. Murphy and B. Van Iersel (New York: Herder and Herder, 1972) 21-34.

describes contemporary ministries as "built upon the apostles," whereas the previous generation had spoken of the apostles as "built upon the Lord." Thus we now have three levels: first the Lord, then the apostles, then those who built upon the apostles — a development which testifies to the concern for continuity.

The pastoral epistles are a major source of information concerning the tensions existing between subapostolic Christian communities and their ministers. What was at stake was the quality of ministry. The Pauline writer states more than once, for example, that Timothy was in continuity with the Lord because when hands were laid upon him he was filled with the Holy Spirit. Yet the same writer does not hesitate to say that even if at one time a minister did receive the Spirit, this does not mean that he has been so ontologically changed that the Spirit will always be at his fingertips, even when he is no longer a Spirit-filled person.[6]

What about flexibility? Again we can look to the pastoral epistles. The time is that of the late subapostolic Church; the places concerned are the city of Ephesus and the island of Crete. The two were as different as any contemporary parishes could be. Ephesus was a large and ancient city. It was an international port and consequently the home of a cosmopolitan and diversified community. The Christians shared this diversity of backgrounds. It is clear, too, that there was a highly developed variety of ministries in the Ephesian church, as is indicated by the way the writer speaks of ministry. In Crete, on the other hand, the situation was entirely different. It was an island in the middle of the Mediterranean which had only recently been evangelized and so had as yet but a small Christian community. The needs of these few Christians were fairly simple, so there was no complex ministerial structure. Here we see the flexibility of the subapostolic Church. We do not find them saying, "Well, if Paul did it that way in Ephesus, that's the way we have to do it

6. J. Meir, "Presbyteros in the Pastoral Epistles," *Catholic Biblical Quarterly* 35 (1973) 323–45.

in Crete." On the contrary, practice was shaped by the needs of the community.

In conclusion, we might mention St. Ignatius of Antioch, a man whose reputation has sometimes suffered because he is alleged to have invented the monarchical episcopate! It is true that his letters, written around the turn of the first century, give us our earliest evidence of communities ruled by a single man. Nevertheless, it is historically certain that at the same time Ignatius was organizing his church under episcopal government at Antioch, the Roman community still had a collegial ministry and had not yet moved to elect a monarchical bishop. Besides, it should also be said that Ignatius was clearly a man of both strength and holiness and that it was his personal charism as much as anything, operating in a community with weak collegial leadership, which unified and vitalized the church there under his leadership.

Still it remains true that in most of the churches to which Ignatius wrote while on his way to martyrdom in Rome, there seems to have been collegial leadership rather than a single bishop at the head of the community. The scholarly work of McCue and Legrand has revealed an interesting detail in Ignatius's letters.[7] Although it is Ignatius who says that the bishop must preside at the Eucharist, the Greek text seems open to the interpretation that, if the bishop does not himself preside for any reason, he may appoint anyone else to take his place—not necessarily someone who belongs to the presbyterate. Such freedom seems, in any case, to have been exercised until the end of the subapostolic period.

What are we to make of such evidence? It suggests, in the first place, that for the first one hundred and twenty-five years, the Church had no blueprint for ministries. Yet it continued to be both creative and flexible, maintaining contact with the Risen

7. J. McCue, "Bishops, Presbyters, and Priest in Ignatius of Antioch," *Theological Studies* 28 (1967) 828-34; H-M. Legrand, "The Presidency of the Eucharist," *Worship* 53 (1979) 413-38.

Lord in deeply symbolic ways that would continue to speak to succeeding generations. Since ministry was there to serve, the Church felt free to tailor ministries to the particular needs of communities, whether they were local churches or missionary areas.

Today the question of what constitutes continuity with the past is once again problematic. A contemporary discussion of ordination in terms of matter and form, for example, is inadequate. Such discussion would use a thirteenth-century theory of sacramentality to grapple with the problems of twentieth-century ministry. The real question that has to be faced concerning ministry is still the one first posed in the early Church: Where is the real continuity with the Risen Christ to be found?

There is also the matter of flexibility. It is a fact that, at the present time, more than a third of the parishes of France are without the ministry of a priest and without any likelihood of obtaining a priest in the foreseeable future. It is also a fact that the bishops of France have designated laymen and laywomen to assume virtually all the functions of a priest except the celebration of the Eucharist and confession.[8] In Bolivia there is a similar situation, and lay leaders are doing more, if anything, than their counterparts in France. In both these cases we need to ask whether such developments are faithful or unfaithful exercises of the Church's freedom to shape its own ministry. Is it not exactly in line with the kind of flexibility found in the churches of Ephesus and Crete, Jerusalem and Corinth? This is not to open the door to all sorts of irresponsible misuses of freedom, but simply to argue as a theologian that the Church has much more freedom in this matter than it usually exercises. That judgment is based both on a historical study of the development of ministries and on theological reflection upon the purpose of ministry in the Church. In short, the claim that existing models of ministry are

8. M. Brulin, "Sunday Assemblies without a Priest in France," Concilium 133 (see note 1) 29-36.

unchangeable cannot be based upon the evidence of the New Testament.

II. THE CATECHUMENAL MODEL

The guidelines of flexibility and the continuity which we have been describing may sound rather utopian in terms of today's Church, at least until we recognize that many of the problems facing ministry today are precisely those of the second and third centuries of Christianity. In those days, the causes of the problems were a persecuted Church and the very complexity and cultural diversity of the different pastoral situations. Moreover, in inviting people to join the Church, Christians were not asking them simply to say "I believe" after thirty minutes of *kerygma*, but to undergo a total change of values, interests, life-styles, and commitments, to the point where they would be prepared not only to go to Mass on Sunday, but to be fed to the lions in the arena on Monday. It is a tribute to the success of the pastoral effort of the churches of the second and third centuries that even toughened Roman soldiers, who had grown up and lived with a totally pagan attitude towards life, were prepared to go into the amphitheater at Rome or Antioch and die for the faith after only two or three years of Christian formation, many of them still unbaptized catechumens.

Perhaps the first thing that needs to be said about the catechumenal model of ministry is that it involves *praxis*. It is not a new program or office to be opened in the chancery. It is not a new course of instructions for non-Catholics. Such shared ministry rather hearkens back to what Augustine said of his own parish: "It is the whole Church that begets each and every Christian." The parish is a begetting community: the catechumenal model takes this not as a theory but as a statement of fact.[9]

The catechumenate, clearly, consists of a core group of Christians who show others, by the way they live and pray, how

---

9. I have developed this idea and the commitment context of all sacraments in a forthcoming book, *Real Presence* (Harper & Row).

to become Christians. When I worked with the catechumenal team at St. Séverin, it was a team composed of both clergy and laypeople from the various parishes. Basically, what we all did was to go through a five-to-seven-year process with the catechumens. It took as long as seven years for some of them to be ready to receive the sacraments of initiation. The reason for this was quite simply that we found, as we prayed upon the gospel together, that the Lord in fact began to demand commitments which we would not have chosen — commitments based, incidentally, on the very talents he gave us in creating us. The word "commitment" comes from the Latin *com* and *mittere.* It means going or sending forth together. This suggests what experience confirms, namely, that both psychologically and spiritually we need others who share our commitment if we are to maintain it. So commitment is a way of going with others. (The gospel life is described in Acts as "the way.")

The kinds of commitment that are evoked in the catechumenate are of such a profound yet practical nature that they go to the very root of our living. For example, in the third-century *Apostolic Tradition,* we are given a list of professions and livelihoods which have to be abandoned by a person who would become a catechumen. Some of these are not surprising: one cannot be a catechumen and continue as a pimp or a prostitute. But it also rules out teaching because in the Roman Empire schooling consisted of the study of the ancient myths, which were considered the enemy of the gospel. Catechumens could not continue to serve as magistrates, for the magistrate was under pressure to act unjustly and, at times, to impose the death penalty.

Catechumenal commitment demands a redefinition of service and values. This is where the image of playing musical chairs becomes useful. In musical chairs, if ten people are playing, they use only nine chairs. While the music plays, everyone continues to move: as soon as it stops, there is a rush to claim the available chairs. The one without a chair drops out, and the music sets everyone on the move again. The players make a tremendous effort to get a chair to sit on, and soon they must get up again, abandon the security of their chairs, and move on. In the catechumenate, the Spirit gathers people who are serious about sharing the gospel. He enables them to leave their false security and to move on in their lives.

Perhaps an illustration will serve to make the point. I was sitting with the catechumens at one evening session and saw in front of me a man who was about thirty-eight years old. I knew something of his past: he had had a fine career, but his whole upbringing and life-style was totally irreligious, just as pagan as the background of the Roman soldier in that North African courtroom seventeen centuries previously. But, in the course of three years' association with the catechumenate, he had been completely turned around. The result was that the rest of us, confronted by his commitment, were forced to question our own. When he started to see what was at stake in his life and began to redefine his own needs and purposes, he forced us, ever so gently, to do the same for ourselves. We all had to leave the security of our chairs. In coming into our Christian community, he began to minister to us. It was not his intention; it was simply the effect of the catechumenal community.

To be converted is to learn to minister to others. The great Scripture scholar Ernst Käsemann once remarked that the New Testament teaching on conversion can be summed up in a single phrase: we shall find our salvation in saving others. In other words, we shall be ministered to only if we are ministers in our turn. There are, for example, many psychologically broken men in the priesthood today: they are broken, not because they are flawed or inadequate to start with, but because they were taught only to minister to others and never to receive the ministrations of others.

The catechumenal model of ministry, therefore, is one that challenges any group of so-called Christians: "You claim to be Christian, but are you a community?" "By this all shall know that you are my disciples, if you have love one for another" (John 13:35). The catechumenate challenges a community of Christians to beget one another in more profound ways: that is, to redefine old needs and to call for new commitments. An example of what I mean: what can be done with a seventy-year-old woman in a parish? Is a lifetime of waiting for the kingdom of God to be rewarded with membership in the senior citizens' club? Are the sacraments to be "applied" to her like some ecclesial Bufferin before the final Great Sleep? What the catechumenate does is to ask every Christian, whatever one's age or condition: "Are you ministering in accordance with the gifts you have at this stage of life? Are you adjusting to the new needs of your parish community?"

Someone who has reached the age of seventy, living in the same parish, perhaps, for half a century or more, has seen many changes in the needs of the parish. Who should be in a better position to minister than one who has lived the Christian life for seventy years, if only the person's gifts could be employed in suitable forms of ministry? It is here that the catechumenate starts, for it is utterly arrogant of us to presume to receive non-Catholics into what is effectively a non-community when we have no place for a seventy-year-old woman who has been a daily communicant for a lifetime. We have to start with the Christians we have and with their ministries. If we cannot cultivate and employ their gifts for service, we have no business adding more dead bodies to the congregation.

Another parable from *Peanuts* sheds light on the concluding point of this section. In one strip, Snoopy lies on top of his doghouse, working on his famous book of theology. Charlie Brown, bringing out his supper, sees him at it and says, "By the way, Snoopy, I have a great quotation for your book from the Bible." Without even asking him for the quotation, Snoopy looks down and says, "Now what would a waiter know about theology?" Whether Schultz knew it or not, the Latin word for "waiter" is "minister." We speak of ministers and ministry because the Lord Jesus taught us that his disciples would be characterized, as he was, by their dedication to service of others. Luke puts this lesson of service right into the context of the Last Supper, where he recounts the dispute which broke out among the followers of Jesus about which of them was the greatest. Jesus cuts through the nonsense: "Who in fact is the greater — he who reclines at table or he who serves the meal? Is it not the one who reclines at table? Yet I am in your midst as the one who serves you" (22:27).

Our problem is that we have not taken seriously this need to serve. Good people have been allowed to go off and practice their religion privately in good conscience. The general commitment to ministry in a parish is the only way this can be avoided — a kind of constant musical chairs going on in the community, where we draw out each other's gifts and respond to one another's needs, having the courage to abandon the security of our chairs because we know that this is how the Christian game is played. And that is how parish community is built up in turn: by its members being converted, not simply to their own private salvation, but to minister to the needs of others.

III. Criteria for Ministry

By way of conclusion, I would suggest four criteria for new ministry.

1. Needs Assessment

The first step in developing new ministries in a parish must be the establishment of a realistic profile of the community's needs. An affluent suburban community, for example, has needs that are rather different from those of an inner-city parish, and consequently its ministries will be different. Too often, however, in contemporary discussions of ministry, even new ministries, the inherited clerical model is the unacknowledged pattern. The clerical model defines things in terms of the powers of the ordained priest: my mother can cook a meal, but I, as a priest, "can put Jesus in the bread." In looking at the historical and catechumenal models, however, we see that ministry is based not on what we *do*, but on what we *are*, in connection with the Risen Lord. If that connection is not visible in our lives—if we are not, in Paul's term, an icon of the Risen One—then of what use is our claim to be able to do this or that? Of what use is a valid sacrament if it is not also fruitful?

In this context, we might notice that Vatican II promulgated a very strong message about what the Church means by "participation": it is to be *activa* (active) and *fructuosa* (fruitful). It is precisely for this reason that the first thing we must address is the profile of needs in a community. That means asking such questions as what a seventy-year-old woman is going to need if she is to walk into the kingdom of God and not crawl into it? People like her do not need to be palmed off with "cheap sacraments," but to be confronted with real sacraments. Real sacraments challenge people to use the gifts they have at the age of seventy—gifts they did not have, perhaps, at the age of fifty or in their youth.

There is a wonderful vignette in one of Camus' books, where he describes a visit to the house of a friend. His friend's elderly mother is there and, seeing their lack of religion, she says: "Go off, then, and I'll just sit here and say the rosary for you." What Camus is highlighting is not the problem of the rosary, but the self-righteousness of people who use their own religion to condemn others and not to draw out their gifts. More often than not, we ourselves condemn the elderly to rote acts of devotion simply because we have nothing to offer them. My seventy-seven-year-old mother has so much life in her—if only it could be given an outlet.

The same is sadly true of young people: we do not know how to draw out their gifts either. The problem of confirmation, for example, is not going to be solved, even with the very best intentions, simply by saying that confirmation will be received henceforth at age sixteen instead of age twelve. It could conceivably be a step in the right direction, but being older does not guarantee greater commitment. It is quite possible for a sixteen-year-old to be deeply committed, while a twenty-six-year-old is still playing with toys. The problem is not one of age, therefore, but one of admitting young people to confirmation when the community has done nothing to elicit any commitment from them. Commitment here does not mean visiting a hospital once in the course of preparing for confirmation to see how the poor people suffer. Instead, we need the catechumenal process, which is supposed to be operative at confirmation as well as at baptism. It is irresponsible to celebrate the sacraments of initiation when we have not troubled to invite the candidates to deeper commitment.

I realize the problems associated with refusing the sacraments and what a delicate pastoral issue that is. The noncelebration of a sacrament can be motivated not simply by the lack of preparation in the candidate, but by the unpreparedness of the ministering community. The question of sacrilegious administration of the sacraments is at stake here. What does sacrilege mean if not being irresponsible in the use of a sacramental sign, knowing that in this situation the recipients are not prepared to receive the sacrament in a way that is honest and true. All I am suggesting is that we remain true to that theology.

It should be clear, then, that my first criterion — that we need to assess the community's needs realistically — refers not simply to the physical and material needs of the parish. It is not simply a matter of getting people to volunteer for bingo. It is a matter of recognizing that at different stages of life people have different gifts, but they fail to recognize them. They have something to give, and they have a need to serve, but they are not asked. A new ministry is awaiting them, but no one has ever told them it was there.

2. Ministries Shaped by People's Commitments

It follows from what has just been argued that ministries must be shaped to people's commitments. That does not usually happen because we tend to think of ministry in functional terms. The dominance of the clerical model can lead us to see everything related to ministry in terms of who can *do* what. We have already seen that ministry is not to be identified with *doing* things: the more basic issue is that of commitment.

This confusion of the question is one of the great problems attending, for example, the diaconate program in this country. Frankly, in many dioceses it is a disaster, not simply because of the type of people being recruited, but because of the kind of training program they are offered. New deacons are simply being told, "Now you can do some of the things that the priest does, but there are other things you can't do because you are not a priest." This is an example of thinking within a functional model. What we need to think about is a ministry shaped by a commitment, which, as we have seen, is shaped in turn by the discovery of one's (sometimes unexpected) giftedness.

Perhaps we can illustrate that by reference to a question that I was asked to address in this paper: Is there no room for passive participation in the parish community? The term "passive participation" can be looked at from two angles: from the viewpoint of the passive parishioner and from that of the parish community.

If "passive participation" means that Christians can sit on their hands and be rewarded by God for doing so, then there is no place for this model in the Church. Such people would be irresponsible in their use of the sacraments. We cannot passively enter into the death and resurrection of Jesus, which is what the sacraments celebrate. The sign that we really share in the death and resurrection of Jesus is that we keep picking up the pieces of our lives for the sake of others. If we are not willing to do that, or if we are willing to do it only up to a certain point, or until we reach a certain age, then there is something radically wrong with the way we are appropriating the gospel.

On the other hand, from the point of view of the community, if there are people who do not seem to be contributing anything to the life of the community, is this lack of participation the result of the existing patterns of ministry in that parish? Perhaps we are ministering to people in such a way that they see themselves simply as objects of our ministry and never think that they, too, might be called to minister. Let us take a "secular" example. There are many women in this country who have undergone a mastectomy for breast cancer. Once the operation is over and they have more or less recovered physically, they are sent home to get on with life as best they can. Hospitals are now saying to such women, "Look, we have a ministry for you. We want you to go and talk to women who are preparing to have this operation. You are the only ones who know what it is really like, and you know the fear that afflicts them." At a stroke, a new ministry is created. These people were capable of exercising that ministry, but they had no chance until someone realized their gift and called it forth.

Transfer this same pattern to the sacramental situation. Here there is a sixteen-year-old who wants to go to Communion — what do we ask of this person? A state of grace? And what does that mean? In asking to go to Communion, that sixteen-year-old is asking to share in the death and resurrection of the Lord. What service can we call forth from him or her? There must be a commitment appropriate to the gifts and abilities of that age, or the person will never grow up. Ministry must be tailored to people's commitment.

3. Different Kinds of Ministry

To speak of ministry is to speak, as we noted earlier, of the two classical levels of ministry: missionary and local. The term "missionary" refers here, not to foreign missions, but to mission within a group of parishes. Missionary ministry means that a group of parishes share their resources — not only their financial resources, but, above all, their gifted people. For example, our catechumenate in Paris, in the deanery of the Latin Quarter, drew on the personal resources of five city parishes. We were able to assemble an excellent catechumenal team because this team effort was seen by participants as a common missionary venture, drawing them out of their parochialism into a broader understanding of Church.

The same principle operates at other levels too. Why is it that young Mennonites, young Mormons, young Baptist men and women who are destined for a professional career can nevertheless be called more easily to missionary service than Roman Catholics? We, as a Church, may be true, but we are not always apostolic. Commitments take many shapes. It may well be that the day when missionary work could confidently be left to religious priests, sisters, and brothers is now over. The day has certainly arrived for people in local parishes to look beyond the narrow horizons of their own turf. For example, in the context of the sacrament of confirmation, what kinds of missionary service could we envisage for a given group of parishes? (For example, the people who mix most easily and speak most forcibly to young people are young people themselves. How often do we call our young people to be youth ministers?) The problem, as always, is how to inspire people to these forms of service, whether missionary or local. We can begin by recognizing the diversity of gifts and needs.

4. Households of Faith

This final point concerns what, in the New Testament, are called the households of faith. Marriage encounter and the charismatic movement have taught us to appreciate that the Lucan descriptions of early Christian living need not have been merely a piece of idealizing fiction. In all the major cities of this country there are flourishing households of faith—family-based ecclesial communities. Of course, such a structure is not without its problems, but we should ask, nonetheless, whether there might not be something we can learn from it. In Kansas, the Capuchins, for example, have a marvellous team ministry which has developed through modular households of faith. Far from destroying the unity of the parish, these family-based cells build it up. Here, and in other similar experiments, we see that we cannot minister, even with a fine pastoral team, to every member of a twelve-hundred-family parish. We were not meant to, nor are we called to do so. On the contrary, we who are ministers must call forth others' ministries.

At this point, it might be objected that we have covered too much ground without actually getting down to naming possible new ministries. That is deliberate. In fact, to attempt to identify new ministries before their emergence in particular situations would not only be presumptuous but would fly in the face of all that we have argued in this paper. I could give—and have given—examples of new ministries in parishes where I have worked, but this tells us nothing about what might emerge in another parish where the needs are different. This variety and flexibility really has to be taken seriously, even to the point where, in certain cases, the people who preside over the Eucharist in different parishes might be different, the people who are called to preach might be different, the forms of service might be different in each community.

I would be reluctant to believe that there is any parish in these United States where the pastoral situation is so bad that what a Paul or a Titus or a Timothy did for their community could not also be done there.

# III. CASES OF PARISH LIFE AND WORSHIP

The Urban Church

EDWARD M. MILLER

St. Bernardine's is a black urban parish in northwest Baltimore. As a parish priest there, I share the work of shepherding the flock with our pastor, Jesus Christ.

As ministers of God's people, we should be engaged in the struggle to fulfill the prayer of Jesus at the Last Supper: that not one given him by his Father should be lost. It is easy enough to identify with the father of the prodigal son. He had lost 50 percent of his family: a 50 percent loss is enough to concern anyone. On the other hand, it is hard to get worked up over the plight of the woman who had lost one of her ten coins: keeping hold on 90 percent of what one has is not bad. But we have a shepherd who, if he loses just one out of a hundred sheep, is prepared to leave the ninety-nine and search for the one that is lost. For him, 99 percent success is not enough. Do we share that zeal?

It is my conviction that vibrant urban churches can and do exist and that they can serve as models for the whole Church in the areas of service, outreach, and celebration. The reflections that follow are the fruit of ten years of ordained ministry and four years of unordained ministry as a seminarian, all in black urban parishes in northwest Baltimore. I would like to begin by

---

EDWARD MILLER is pastor of St. Bernardine Church in Baltimore. He has served as director of the Archdiocese of Baltimore Urban Commission and founded the St. Ambrose Housing Aid Center. His entire priestly ministry has been spent in a black urban setting.

describing one of those urban church families, the family of St. Bernardine's, a parish that refused to die.

I. St. Bernardine's, Baltimore

In 1975 St. Bernardine's was a parish of about 250 members and was dwindling. The school had closed in 1973, with the added irony that the parish inherited not one but two school buildings —so large had the parish been at one time. A convent that had housed twenty nuns was rented to a concern that sold food stamps. One of the school buildings was rented to a private day care center, while the other school had become a small black Protestant church. The black community was saying something about its needs in all this and how St. Bernardine's was not meeting them.

It is also ironic that the emblem for this Conference on the parish is Noah's ark. Just as Noah sent the animals in two by two, so God sent a pair of priests—but being Catholic, of course, God had to send two males this time! Fr. Maurice Blackwell had been assigned to the parish in June 1974. He was black and newly ordained. I came in June 1975, replacing the priest who had been pastor. We were both twenty-nine years of age, and having two young men assigned to a parish was unheard of in Baltimore. We agreed that I had more pastoral experience, but that he had more experience in the black community, so together we set out to form a team ministry.

We had one advantage. At twenty-nine, we were clearly not there to preside over a sinking ship, nor to close the parish down. The parish was ill, certainly; and like a patient who, wanting to die, refuses to eat, so the parish seemed gripped by a death-wish. A baby will die if it is not touched and hugged and fed and loved—and the parish was dying. But what did Martha and Mary do when Lazarus fell sick? They sent for Jesus, the doctor who never lost a patient. Accordingly, we felt that worship was vital if the parish was to live. We were, after all, a *church,* a fact that gave us our meaning. The community was black, and that indicated the direction to go in its style of worship. We had to visit other black churches to listen to the preachers; we had to listen to the people; we had to read; we had to be open to learn. We made use of Henry Mitchell's classic book on black preaching; of the music of Fr. Clarence Rivers; of the offerings of the National Office of Black Catholics; of the ministry of black preachers. We knew some things, had some hunches, grew a lot.

Why do people come to the Church? *To get in touch with God, to feel God!* In the black community, there is a phrase: "to *have* church," that is, the feeling that God is with you, that you have touched him, that he has touched you. It has not been unusual for black Catholics "to go to Mass" out of a sense of obligation and then, later in the day, to go to a black Protestant church just down the street and "have church." We bemoan the excuses people offer for not coming to church: "I can find God anywhere" or "I can pray in my room" or "God is with me in my heart." "True," people who come to church might say, "but we can't limit God." People who come to church would tell us that they want to get in touch with God in the church, in the family of believers. They thereby pay us a compliment, but they will vote with their feet if we do not deliver. Our worship, our spirituality, must touch them. Our congregation, being black, was telling us that worship had to be alive, filled with the Spirit of God.

There are five elements in black worship that I will discuss briefly: music, prayer, preaching, time, and expression.

1. Music. We hired a black man, a young Baptist, as our minister of music. (Later he became a Catholic and joined the church.) We taught him Catholic liturgical principles and sent him to the N.O.B.C. workshop on Afro-American Worship and Culture. (He now serves on the faculty of the N.O.B.C. worship workshops!) In the parish he formed a gospel choir. For some parishioners, this took some getting used to: they had to work the idea through. We did not ram it down anyone's throat: blacks are not more monolithic than whites, and not all our parishioners, even now, come to the gospel choir liturgy. A parish needs pluralism.

We often bemoan the fact that only 4 percent of the black population is Catholic, but what was happening in our parish? Blacks came to our church for the social services that we provided: for food, for help with an eviction or a gas and electric turn-off notice, for schooling. But the important point is that they were not coming to "get over." They were genuinely grateful that the Church cared in these areas. Still, on a Sunday, those same people would go down the street to First Baptist Church. Why? Because four hymns and a three-minute sermon did not meet their spiritual need. It was not enough just to have all the various liturgical ministries properly filled. The answer did not lie in the areas of art, music, and vestments; in making banners and training lay people; in having women in the sanctuary and English in the liturgy. People wanted to get in touch with God; with the God who woke them up this morning, who breathed life into them, who kept them safe all week: "My soul looks back and wonders how I got over." They wanted to get in touch with a God who is ready, willing, and able to "deliver me right now," with a God who did it—he did not have to, but he did it anyway—for Moses, for David, for Shadrack, Mishack, and Abednago. People want to feel that "as long as I've got King Jesus, don't need nobody else." There are too many churches in our urban areas that compete with the Department of Social Service, yet fail to touch the people in terms of worship.

2. Prayer at Mass. This is above all the priest's role—and it means more than being able to read well. Our opening prayer, formerly known as the collect, does what its ancient name suggests: it collects the prayers of the people, gathers them up, and hands them to the Lord. But most of the opening prayers in our sacramentary are sterile; they are just dry bones. The role of the priest as *pray-er* is to put flesh on these dry bones, to breathe life into them. This requires preparation, meditation on the theme of the liturgy of the day, and a knowledge of what is happening in the life of the community.

3. *Preaching.* If a priest meets a child, especially an unchurched child, on our city streets, the child will probably ask him, "Are you a preacher?" As it is taught in our seminaries, preaching focuses on one idea and is supposed to last no more than three to five minutes. "The people won't listen if you are long," seminarians are told. I believe that this is the biggest deception in our training. Whether we usually agree with Andrew Greeley or not, his constant complaints about poor Catholic preaching are right on target. Our people are hungry for good biblical preaching.

Jesus was a preacher, he told stories well; and we can do it, using the Scripture passages given in our lectionary. It will take some preparation and a few hours' hard work every week, but the people are hungry. There is such a richness in the Scriptures, especially in the Old Testament; though I must admit that my favorite Old Testament story is from 2 Kings 2:23-24, where Elisha is returning to Bethel and the children taunt him for being a bald-headed man. Elisha calls down a curse on them, with the result that two bears come and devour all forty-three of them!

Preaching is not a lecture. In the black community someone may remark, "I've heard him speak," but that does not mean that the person preached.

4. *Time.* A lady called me one Sunday and asked, "What time is your last Mass?" When I told her, she then inquired, "And when will it be over?" I replied, "When the Holy Ghost has had his say." So many of our sister parishes in the suburbs are scheduled for Sunday Masses by St. McAdam, the patron saint of parking lots. It is one of the advantages of our urban churches that we do not have to worry about parking lots: our worship can be open-ended.

5. *Expression.* It is not unusual to hear someone shout "Amen!" or for someone to "get their shout in," or even for some-

one to dance in the aisle. The prayerful sound of "Amazing Grace" may cause some to throw up their hands and shout, "Thank you, Jesus!" when they understand that "he saved a wretch like me." A "call to worship" at the beginning of the Mass or a chance for a person to come and give "testimony" or respond to an "altar call" are also quite frequent. We need such freedom of expression and freedom from the rigidity of the Roman Rite if the liturgy is to take on its fullest expression.

II. What Makes Liturgy Work?

We have all had experiences where the gospel has proved to be too close to real life for our comfort: experiences such as that described in Matthew 22, where the king prepared a glorious supper, and none of those invited came. We may have a parish with good quality liturgy and skilled professionals in every ministry and find that no one is coming. For a parish really to have good liturgy, three things must converge: [1] the ability to celebrate liturgy well, which will *shape* the parish family; [2] a spirit of evangelization, so that parishioners may get to know one another and *grow together* as family; [3] living service, so that the parish family might become a *caring* family. These three dimensions are essential not only for urban parishes but for all our parishes.

When people think of the urban parish, they often think in terms of a "ghetto." But I would like to suggest that the suburban parish is really a "ghetto church" if it is weak in the area of service, if it is concerned with "Catholics only," if the liturgy is on a forty-five-minute schedule, and if the parishioners are merely "strangers in the night" to one another.

The institutional Church seems content to play the "numbers game" with the urban church. Clergy assignments are made on the basis of the number of Catholics in the area, rather than on mission considerations. It seems to be a matter of nuts-and-bolts maintenance, of mere survival. This may sound like a simplistic generalization, but the fact is that there are very few suburban churches that are vital or innovative. I recognize that there are the problems of sheer numbers of people to be served and jobs to be done: trying to get weekend help; dealing with First Communions, weddings, and funerals; coping with the "masses" and the "Masses." But if it is a question of heartburn or heart attack, which requires more and immediate attention?

The institutional Church is concerned with maintaining "Catholic life," while the urban churches are concerned with the terrors of death: with poor urban education, with high school graduates too illiterate to read their diplomas; with drugs, the poison of the community; with housing deterioration and with local inspectors who are on the take; with police-and-community relations and the racism which exists in so many police forces; with the lack of jobs which is tearing our families apart. It may be cute to see father and son wearing matching T-shirts; it may be cute to see a three-year-old wearing the word **UNEMPLOYED** across his chest; but it is no joke on a twenty-five-year-old father.

When there is a large parish that has to be "taken care of," it is hard to be concerned with outreach and evangelization, with social justice and social action. Justice then becomes simply a sermon topic when it is time to collect money for the Campaign for Human Development. How many churches prayed for the victims of Mount St. Helens? But how many also prayed for the victims of the Miami rioting, or for Vernon Jordan when he was gunned down, or for those killed in Atlanta? We must realize that an urban parish is defined, not in terms of the number of *Catholics* there, but of the number of *people* in that community. So many are lost, so many do not know Jesus, so many do not know any personal dignity—they know everything that dehumanizes. For city people, urban renewal has meant nothing more than urban *removal:* the great melting pot has become the new American dumping ground.

And I hear Jesus read from a scroll: "The Spirit of the Lord is upon me. He has sent me to preach the good news to the poor."

Jesus preached not just in the pulpit, but in the streets; not just with words, but with signs. Where there was sickness, there was now cure; where there was water, there was now wine; where there was a loaf, there was now a feast; where there was death, there was now life. This continued to amaze people. It even amazed John the Baptist so much that Jesus had to send word to him, "What did you expect to see?" And I know *why* the urban church is involved in housing, drug treatment, food distribution, prison ministry, even offering our old convents or other buildings as community correction centers, with the incarcerated literally becoming our neighbors. Were not the poor the ones who were most receptive to Jesus? *And the poor have long memories.*

A church of service and outreach into the community is there to break bread and to share it. As people see this, they ask, "Why? Why are you like this? Why do you live this way? Who or what is it that inspires you? Why are you here?" Our answer is that we are not here to "get" them, but to *help* them. We play an instrument of justice, an instrument whose sound is on key, in an orchestra of urban chaos and cacophony. We are messengers of love, asking not, "Are you a Catholic?" but, "How can we serve you?" Our love for the people and our service in the community attract attention, gain respect, and invite inspection.

Service and evangelization go hand in hand. Pope Paul VI remarked in his exhortation *Evangelii nuntiandi* that evangelization is "to affect and upset, if needs be, through the power of the gospel, mankind's criteria of judgment, determining values, points of interest, lines of thought, sources of inspiration, and models of life which are in contrast with the word of God and the plan of salvation." So many of our parishes will never be strong, evangelizing communities because they are ghettos. They are not out in the marketplace; they are "for Catholics only."

A church that is alive in worship, touching God in prayer and praise, serving him through service to our brothers and sisters, will be an *evangelizing* parish because it is "for real." It is making a statement to those outside, to those who suffer, that "God made me and God doesn't make junk!" And it will also be an *evangelized* parish, as its members deepen their realization of what they are doing and why they are doing it. In this context, we should notice something that is a very real danger in the contemporary Church, namely, that evangelization becomes identified simply with parish renewal. If we think we have to wait for a parish to become what it ought to be before we begin to move towards evangelization, we shall become stuck in the kind of parish renewal which is merely an exercise in "navel-gazing."

At St. Bernardine's, the staff began to set an example. Throughout the community, we would act as servants, we would be with the people, whether they were Catholic or not. We would try to show that we cared and then, through our example, we hoped, the parish family would begin to show concern for one another and for the wider community. This involved, of course, learning about the needs of the larger community. For example, in our black community it was clear that the young people constituted a primary area for ministry. Whereas the median age of black citizens in this country is twenty, the median age of black Catholics is about fifty-two; so it was obvious that youth ministry had to become a priority. But, to attract young people, the local church does not have to give itself over entirely to the youth culture. Rather, we have to take young people seriously and learn to integrate them into the mainstream of life in the Church. After all, the same Jesus who attracted Peter also attracted John.

At the same time, in our preaching we emphasized evangelization, reminding the people that they knew who had stopped coming, who in their own families used to come but came no more, who on their block was looking for a church family. We reminded them that it could not be left to two priests to make the parish grow. People on the job discuss religion and politics: when that happens, why not invite them to church one Sunday?

However, I do believe that the largest challenge facing the Church today is to answer the question, what are we inviting the people to come to? The Rite for the Christian Initiation of Adults (R.C.I.A.) does not provide the answer simply by itself; this leads me to mention five concerns I have in this area.

1. No rite, by itself, has the power to "turn people on." The R.C.I.A. is no exception to this principle.

2. If we think of the purposes of the R.C.I.A. as being to produce a group of super Christians, we are in danger of introducing a double standard into the community. We already have pews full of sheep who are not being fed, who often do not even know they are hungry — and some of them are hardly aware that they are in a pew!

3. We must ask ourselves what kind of Church we are asking people to join. Is it a family? Is it a powerhouse of prayer? Is it a living Christ who loves and serves the poor? Is it a zealous Church, eager to reach out to the unchurched? When we manage to lay aside our rhetoric, is this a realistic description of how our parish functions?

4. We have been taught — and rightly so — that law should be kept to a minimum. Are we now introducing a new legalism with all our "requirements" and "guidelines," making a new class of super Catholics and weeding out the weak? Under the guise of challenging people, are we in fact denying them their chance? Yet, who is it that needs the physician, the healthy or the sick? What value does reflecting on the image of the "broken vessel" — with Jesus picking up the pieces — have for Catholics implementing the R.C.I.A.?

5. I would suggest that all talk about "the faithful remnant" be rejected if the image is used to suggest that our goal should be to have just a few faithful people remaining in the Church.

Turning to the practice of evangelization, we deliberately set out at St. Bernardine's to use some rather simple ideas. We publicized our existence by means of a parish newsletter, buttons, T-shirts, mugs, rented billboards, reports in both the secular and the Catholic press, and even a record album made by the choir. People have to know that a parish is alive, or else they will assume that it is dead. (This point was vividly brought home to me when I took a bulk mailing to the post office and the postman remarked, "I thought your church was closed." I knew that when the mailman thinks you are closed, you are in real trouble!)

From the pulpit we proclaimed that we would never preach on money matters, only on the Scriptures. "If we are doing what we should be," we told the parishioners, "then you support us with your fair share; and if we are not, then help change things or stop supporting us." How many parishes could risk making that kind of statement? How many would find it a prelude to a severe drop in its revenues? Yet we went from a parish requiring an annual subsidy of $24,000 to a parish that needed no subsidy at all — all in a period of just four years.

Our choir went out to sing, surprising many people who never thought that a Catholic parish would have a gospel choir. Often, one of the priests would go along with them, thereby giving us a chance to pray before or during the concert. We also made a point of using the parish bulletin to advertise where the choir would be appearing, so that our people could go along and support them.

There were other things that we did. If there was no news, we made news. We would try anything. We challenged our people too: "God wants to use you to do great things." It worked with Abraham and Moses, why not with our people? But we also told our people how much we enjoyed being with them as their shepherds. Our people feed us continually, yet we priests never tell them that or thank them for it. We celebrate everything and anything, knowing that where there is life there will be pride. Was anyone ever heard to say, "Hey, you ought to come to my church, it's really dead!"

III. Catechumenate

The catechumenate is a vital part of a living, worshiping church, but there are several lessons that experience has taught us.

1. It must be advertised. It is essential to keep the parish informed of what is happening and to let parishioners witness the life and growth that take place.

2. It must be adapted. The Rite for the Christian Initiation of Adults was not written with the American church specifically in mind. For one thing, it supposes that the catechumens are coming from paganism, whereas our experience has chiefly been with people who already know Jesus, but have no idea of the Catholic Church.

3. It must be flexible. Fixing a timetable of eighteen months for everyone is unrealistic: it assumes we are starting from the beginning with every individual. We need to find the flexibility which will allow us to avoid both the *rigidity* of making everyone serve eighteen months as catechumens and the *laxity* of some pastors who will receive anyone who walks up the aisle into the church.

4. It is advisable to have a parish sponsor for each candidate, as well as the baptismal sponsor chosen by the catechumen. The role of the parish sponsors is to help make the catechumen feel at home in the family of the church, to answer questions, to pray each day for their charge, to ensure that the catechumen is invited to all parish functions and does not stay away because of feeling left out.

5. The rites provided for use at Sunday Mass should be used and adapted. The enrollment, the election, and the scrutinies, celebrated at the Sunday liturgy, tell the parish that there are people who want to join the community. Some parishes dismiss the catechumens after the Liturgy of the Word, as the rite suggests, but we do not. Most of our catechumens have been coming to Mass before they made their decision to seek membership in the Catholic Church.

6. The bishop should be invited for some of the rites—if possible, for the initiation or reception itself. He should see this growth and celebrate it with the parish. It is a qualitatively different experience from the usual confirmation rounds.

7. At St. Bernardine's we have the custom of presenting a Jerusalem Cross to adults we baptize or receive into the Church. This is the Missionary Cross, and it serves as a reminder to them: as someone brought them to the Church, now it is their turn to bring someone else to "taste and see the goodness of the Lord." This also serves to emphasize the role of the people as a whole in the work of evangelization.

8. A service component is necessary in the catechumenate, to challenge the people with ways to serve as members of the Church, besides just coming to Mass on Sundays.

9. Every baptism or reception ends with a party, usually given by the previous catechumenal class.

St. Bernardine's has led the entire archdiocese of Baltimore in converts for the last three years, averaging about seventy a year. Most of these have been relatives and friends of parishioners, and their sponsors, too, have been parishioners—evidence of how the Church as mother continues to give birth. We would like to think that the parish, like the woman at the well (and her sisters in conversion—the woman taken in adultery and the woman at the house of Simon the Pharisee), went running to announce, "Come and see a man who told me everything I have done. Could this be the Messiah?"

IV. Parish Evangelization Committee

Our parish has established an evangelization committee and, again, we use simple ideas to make people aware of the life of the Church—such things as the use of a parish guest book; creation of Visitors' Sunday (with invitations mailed not only to former visitors, but to a blanket section of the parish as well as to people we have been able to help in the area of social services); setting up a parish booth at community festivals; advertising the programs of the church; distributing Scripture tracts (but with no "hard sell"); initiating a week-long parish revival, which includes setting a theme, inviting other churches, organizing a potluck supper to kick it off, and so on. A special project carried out last year was the designation of the month of November as "Try God This Month." A parish covenant was arranged, and parishioners agreed to try to bring someone who was alienated or without a church to call home. Monthly attendance rose an average of fifty persons a week after this program was completed. This requires more than gimmicks: it requires a church that is able to say to those who come, "We are family," and even, "Forgive us." The parish must also be willing to invest in training its members for evangelization, perhaps by sending them to the national training workshops run by the Bishops' Committee on Evangelization. As one of our parishioners reflected one evening, "We've been doing evangelization all our lives and just didn't have a fancy name to call it." St. Bernardine's now has a weekly attendance of 750, and we continue to grow.

Liturgy, service and outreach, evangelization—all these interweave to create a beautiful Joseph's coat called "living Church." It does not happen only in the city but, all things being equal, I see the urban situation offering the best opportunity for it to happen.

As in so much of the Church today, the role of the professional minister in the city parish is crucial. The priest is a leader, setting the tone for the whole parish. I once gave a talk on evangelization in an ethnic parish and, at the end of my remarks, the pastor arose and said that people today were too materialistic and that was why they were not in church. All the enthusiasm that had been building in the audience, all the desire to reach out and share their faith, was destroyed at a stroke by the pastor's remark. The parish priest also has a role as leader of prayer, as celebrant of those acts of the Church which define and create us anew as God's loving and serving people and sustain us in our efforts to live accordingly. But an urban situation demands that that same priest also walk the streets and eat right from the pots on the stoves in people's homes. In short, he must be available and present to his people. Living in the community is a significant advantage. Because we live among our people, we can *live* church; if we traveled in on a Sunday, we could only *hold* church. Full-time ministry is so important because people do not have the luxury of scheduling their crises. But, above all, the priest's ministry must be non-discriminatory, not just for Catholics only.

Some priests are threatened by Robert Schuler and others like him, who are taking over the airwaves and winning converts through the media. But Schuler knows his limitations for, as he once remarked to someone, "You are the pastor. You hold the widow's hand in the cemetery. You hold the dying patient's hand. You counsel the troubled teen. You ensure that the young couple invite Christ to the marriage and not just to the wedding ceremony." Are we not the ones who feed the hungry, clothe the naked, visit the prisons, shelter the homeless, and also celebrate God's love in worship?

We celebrate life liturgically — life that is survival, potential, puzzle; life that is the joy in the morning that every nighttime weeper has felt. There are as many people living in the territory of our city parishes today as there were in the "old days," when our urban parishes were predominantly Catholic. Today our new residents are not primarily Catholic, but they also need the Lord, and their lives are just as precious. There are 5,000 McDonald's in our country, but there are 18,600 Catholic parishes. How sad it is that our young people know more about Ronald McDonald than about Jesus Christ, are more familiar with Big Macs than with the Bread of Life. The best news I can give is news of hope: we *can* do the job. We do not need a lot of money, new buildings, years of experience, or intensive training. What we need, we already have: "Silver and gold I do not have, but what I have I give you" (Acts 3:6). We have people —

people who are in love with Jesus and proud of their church, who are willing to share it, who love to praise God in it, and who are eager to serve God through it. Amen. Amen. Amen.

The Rural Parish

MARY ANN SIMCOE

The root word for "rural" means open land. The open land may be the only element that all rural parishes have in common: open land that separates people, a less dense population. "Rural" is a broad term that includes agriculture, agriculturally-related business and manufacturing, mining, forestry, ranching. My own experiences have been in farming communities, and my comments flow solely from that brand of rural life. Within the agricultural community, rural parishes vary from an isolated church and its cemetery to a full parish complex in towns which are located in the open country but which, due to the presence of industry or a college in the town, are relatively divorced from the farming community which surrounds them. A rural town can have as transient a population as suburbia. The rural parish, then, is not a univocal phenomenon, but a varied one.

Rural parishes as *parishes*, as local living cells of the Church, do not differ greatly from city parishes. They share the same four basic functions: worship, formation, service, and the work of administration which allows the other functions of the Church to flourish. From my point of view as an itinerant

---

MARY ANN SIMCOE is director of the office of liturgy for the diocese of Des Moines, Iowa, and coordinated the celebration of the rural church for the papal Mass in Des Moines. She holds a master's degree in liturgy from Notre Dame and has pastoral experience in Minnesota, Texas, and Iowa. She is a member of the executive board of the Federation of Diocesan Liturgical Commissions.

liturgist, rural parishes cannot be classified on the basis of their liturgical expression. Some of the rural parishes of my diocese have more in common with my parents' suburban parish than with neighboring rural parishes, if the differences and similarities are judged by the presence of competent liturgical ministers or the quality of liturgical planning for the Sunday Eucharist. One pastor with whom I spoke did not see any fundamental difference between urban and rural parishes, although he was raised in a farming community and has served in city and country. When asked what makes a rural parish tick, he responded, "What makes *any* parish tick?" A woman who was raised in the city and now farms with her husband and five children said, "The parish is the same here as anywhere — only more so. The experience of parish life is more intense in a rural community."

The particular blessings and curses of rural parishes arise not because of the life of the church *per se,* but from the life situations and the sociological and geographical features of the rural communities within which they exist. I will first examine three primary relationships that have a key influence on the character of rural parishes and indicate several pastoral challenges which those relationships present and, second, I will discuss some important tools for ministers who are responsible for the liturgical life of the rural parish.

I. Three Primary Relationships

1. Relationship with the Land and God
I can hardly speak of the relationship with God and the land as distinct realities. In my conversations, the two were often spoken of in the same breath. "You establish your relationship with God in the field. It's free, open, flexible. And strong. The land and God are ever-present, everlasting, and intimate," said one. Another witness told me, "There is a stoicism in our people. There's a splendid misery about farming. A love for hanging on

by their teeth. It gives the farmer a unique identity as an oppressed minority that is misunderstood and unappreciated economically."

In their relationship with the land, farmers meet God. The open space and fields are at once a source of intimacy with God and the barrier that physically separates and isolates households from one another. In conversation with a farmer who works the same land his grandfather had farmed, I asked whether he had received the rain that had fallen in the city the night before, whether he would have to replant his crops as the news media were predicting would be necessary if rain did not come soon. "No, no rain," he said, "and that particular seed just sits there and waits. And so do I. You just trust." Another person told me, "God is patient, because they are patient." Lastly, "Eternal rest *means* something in a farming community. You work so hard."

What challenge does the trusting, patient, stoic relationship with the land and the God who created it bring to the minister or pastor in a rural parish? It is to take the overwhelming elements of life, health, the land, and water and to theologize from the intimate experience of them. The root experience of faith and trust is there. God is not the water or the wind, but he is recognized as source of life. The gospel must be brought to life in terms of that experience.

Today we are recovering an understanding of preaching and teaching the gospel by relating the personal story to the salvation story. Can we not speak of Jesus' surrender to death, his passage to life, his trust in the Father's love, and relate that story to the deeply ingrained, rarely spoken, patient, waiting trust that a farming community experiences? To the experiences of economic disaster and destruction of crops that northwest Iowa is experiencing this spring? To the joy of last fall's harvest, the most bountiful harvest in history? Farming is a series of crises from planting, to harvest, to marketing the goods. Both destruction and bounty are out of the farmer's hands. None of us controls life, but in the city, life goes on with a pretense that claims to control the uncontrollable. The farming community also experiences the fragility of life on a regular basis: its seasonal stories of death and life lie in wait for the story of the Good News of the victory of life over death in Christ. Country people know how to be attentive, too. The farmer labors long and hard to make everything ready and then waits at great risk. The natural forces of sun and wind and rain are beyond human control, but they complete the farmer's work. Does that experience not speak of watchfulness for the reign of God?

The one complaint I heard in my rural conversations was that very often what goes on in the life of a rural person is not addressed by preaching. The challenge and opportunity for homilists and teachers to relate the life-experience of rural community to the gospel is enormous!

2. *Relationship with the community*

The unknowns of the farming life and the isolation of households from one another breed a staunch individualism and self-reliance in the people. But the counterpoint to the unknowns and independence of farming life is the strength and closeness of community bonds which exist in the rural setting. I have both experienced and been told of the interdependence between households that makes the community at large an extended family. The community's closeness has both blessings and curses for parish life. My opinion is that the familiarity of the community life tames, balances, and is a refuge from the uncertainty of the occupation. The strength of community bonds is directly related to the unknown of natural forces. The families that comprise a community become survivors together. There is an unspoken solidarity, a unity of spirit, and interdependence because of the life they lead individually. A friend of mine recently told me about her brother and his friend, who had both lost all their hogs. The second man came to the brother's home. All he had to say was: "I knew this would be the best place to come. You'd understand."

Whether or not I have presented a romantic view of the strengthening effects of isolation and potential disaster upon the bonds of rural communities, I do rely on the experiences of the people who told me: "You always, always keep an eye on your neighbor's place, to watch for a fence that's down or sick cattle." "You are more aware of people because there are fewer of them. People are more precious." "Everyone *is* related to everyone, and at least recognized by everyone else." "You are known and you feel the belonging."

All these comments on rural community relationships explain, if there can be an explanation, the most outrageously generous community response I have ever witnessed. While I lived in Minnesota, the home of one of the families burned in a fire so fierce that the house was destroyed before help could arrive for the house or for their youngest son, who died in the blaze. It is true, every parish in which I have lived has responded generously to pleas for help for earthquake victims, resettling refugees, tornado-savaged towns, and every imaginable disaster; but the community's response to the needs of that rural Minnesota family surpassed anything I have ever seen. Anything, everything the family needed, down to shoes in proper sizes for the entire family, was given, was there. No plea for help was needed.

Alongside the positive benefits of close rural community life are the problems. "It's true that you know everyone else's business, not only the present, but the past as well. Your roots and background travel with you into your present relationships in the community." The same familiarity that breeds a sense of belonging can also make peer pressure a major obstacle to freedom and responsibility. Because the communal history usually goes back to the settling of the land, families who have lived in a community for five, ten, or even twenty-five years can be and are referred to as new folks. Individuals often hesitate to step forward to take on a new role, especially a leadership position. A pastor reported that his people simply refused to "excel too much," because they move from their established niches: "You not only may be stepping out of your own comfort zone, but of the community's comfort with you."

Attending church to maintain social respectability is no less a reality in a small rural community than in any other setting. One does not miss Mass when one feels that not only God, but the entire community, numbers every hair on your head and will inquire where you were.

In summary, for better and worse, in a rural community a person is known and also knows who people are and where they come from. As one woman told me: "There's no place to hide."

The stable, rooted, public dimensions of rural-community bonds present challenges for rural ministry. "Rural parishes are so far behind, they are ahead," declared a city dweller who was born a farmer's daughter, "but most of the people I grew up with would take that as an insult, a proclamation that they are backwards. But they need to know and be told that they enjoy what the city and suburban parishes are striving so hard to get. They have the experience but not the reflection and healthy self-awareness of the gifts of their communal life. Rural parishes have a great gift to offer city parishes. Too often the rural parishes have big-city expectations and programs laid upon them, and the rural people get the impression that they are inadequate."

The strength of the community relationships provides a pastoral opportunity to name the unique bond of the rural community and claim it for Christ, to announce that the Good News is present here in our midst, to live and love not in spite of one another, because we know each other too well, but because of one another.

The second challenge results from the dark side of the closeness. The pain and hurt of conflicts and misunderstandings are felt deeply and can become part of the community heritage. In one Texas parish of two hundred people, there is a family feud that is three generations old. That's a critical rift in so small a community.

Within families, long-lasting jealousies are connected with who inherits the family farm. Much of the sense of morality is determined by what enhances or detracts from the family name.

The potential power of reconciliation in a small rural community, sacramental and otherwise, is that much more profound. And the gospel imperative to forgive and accept forgiveness is that much more difficult to speak and to hear.

The third challenge which arises from the self-consciousness that exists in a close-knit community is the constant calling forth of the people's gifts for the good of the community. One pastor said, "It's such a breakthrough to get people to work together on a 'churchy' project. And they work together so well on any other type of project. There's no problem with finances or bazaars or drives for the missions, but when it comes to areas that have formerly been the domain of the priest—liturgy and religious education—somehow it's still the pastor's responsibility." It takes great care and a long time to build the confidence, self-image, and willingness to take the risk of stepping out of old patterns into new ones; and to do so knowing that the community's response may be, "Aren't you Joseph's son? Don't we know who you are supposed to be?"

Finally, I must credit this comment to Fr. Bernard Quinn of Glenmary Research Center, author of *The Small Rural Parish*, published by the National Conference of Catholic Bishops' Committee on the Parish. Father Quinn writes:

> Because of the interlocking relationships, rural ministry requires a communal approach. It is the community as a whole whose influence on the individual is decisive, and whom the individual influences in turn. In serving one person, therefore, ministers will keep one eye on all those cousins, uncles, aunts, acquaintances and associates who are, so to speak, peering over a person's shoulder, and will take them into account.

This insight is not limited to the rural ministry; many pastoral situations call for sensitivity to a person's "community." One keeps the extended family in mind when preparing parents for their child's baptism, or engaged couples for their marriage, or adults for seeking baptism in the Catholic Church. The individual cannot be served in isolation.

3. *Relationship to the Church*

When I had been in the diocese of Des Moines barely a month, I attended a parish function. One of the parishioners to whom I was introduced as the new director of the diocesan liturgy office asked, "Who are you going to work with, the priests or the people?" "A little of each," said I, both in truth and in the hope that my response would satisfy whatever he had in mind. "Well," he responded, "the priests come and go, the people have been here for over a hundred years." That is my most memorable introduction to ministry in southwest Iowa.

Rural communities perceive the church as both "us" and "them." On the "us" side, the church is perceived as the local community and its parish buildings. In the country, people travel miles to shop, to visit, to recreate, but not to worship. Although it may be several miles to their own church, they do not travel miles in the other direction to visit other parishes. I asked one family whether they would go to another parish for "better liturgy." The response was an emphatic *no*. The reason given: it would damage, drain their community to leave it so easily. Furthermore, even in the face of a difficult parish situation, they would remain. This family's attitude reveals a profound sense that their parish is more than Sunday liturgy, more than the presence of a compatible pastor, and greater than the differences between parishioners. The church is the People of God of their particular community. And one worships with one's community.

The identification of the church with the local community can also foster a very narrow vision of the church. In the Minnesota town in which I lived were three parishes, the French, the Irish, and the German, all within the shadow of one another. The same community of sisters operated separate grade schools for each parish. During my time there, these parishes had begun joint operation of a central grade school and religious education program out of economic necessity. After a few years' success with their joint ventures, they had begun to cooperate on other common ventures. Yet, as recently as seven years ago, the term "mixed marriages" was still used to refer to intermarriage between the national groups. The ethnic identity and rivalry blocked the vision of the Church's unity. The same situation often exists among neighboring towns and parishes whether or not they are of different ethnic origin.

The proximity of southern Iowa to the Bible Belt presents another barrier to a Catholic parish's sense of a Church broader than the individual parish. Catholics are a minority in these areas. And the Catholic parishes, surrounded by other congregations which are autonomous and not highly influenced by a strong denominational government, have difficulty understanding why they cannot have the same autonomy with respect to church goals and direction as the other congregations. The vision of the Roman Catholic Church at large is often very limited.

The parish buildings, especially the church itself, are often a key symbol of the rural parish's identity. In an urban or suburban area, the parishioners who built a parish complex may no longer be there, and the current parishioners may have no personal investment in the church furnishings. In a rural parish the population is much more stable. One's family history is often directly linked to the church and its decoration. The church building is a source of pride, especially in ethnic communities that created a replica of a church in the homeland or acquired furnishings from the homeland at great expense. The church witnesses to the sacrifice of ancestors, the love and labor that continues in one's own flesh. The church represents a tradition to be passed on to the next generation.

The church and its school, if it has one, is a social and economic influence on a rural town. When a school closes, if the parish closes, the town will suffer and begin a slow death. Church-related activities bring people to town. The church presence provides a traffic pattern which attracts and maintains local businesses. The presence of the rural church, then, is a source of stability for the entire community.

In summary, in a rural parish, the church is the local community, not the neighboring parish. A sense of the diocese is notably absent. The rural parish's identification with faraway foreign missions is often stronger than the identification with neighboring parishes or the see city.

How is the Church perceived as "them?" This is represented by the presence of a resident pastor and those responsible for sending the pastor. This is not to imply that the pastor remains an outsider or is kept at a distance. On the contrary, pastors who stay aloof and associate with only a few families, or the "leader families," are resented. Nevertheless, the potential loss of a resident pastor is akin to the threat of nuclear war, ever-present but never spoken of. It won't happen to us.

The presence of a resident pastor validates the community's worth. A pastor from southern Illinois described his two parishes to me: one, "the parish," and the other, "the mission." The "mission" people, he said, are a delight to be with; they work twice as hard and enthusiastically as the "parish" people, and they are willing to try anything. These people were compensating for their "mission" status and ensuring that they would not be regarded as a second-rate community.

Regarding the pastors, I was told: "It's the luck of the lottery." My urban experience was much the same, except that the city offers more variety. As I was growing up it was, "Guess who's coming to help with Mass this weekend." However, this does have special ramifications for the rural parish. "There can be so much sameness. When the pastor has been here for several years, you know what he's going to say before he opens his mouth. Where can we go to feed our faith if the present pastor is not meeting our needs?"

A few words from pastors: "There's no room for pretense." "If you gain a parish's trust, you can lead them anywhere." "Up to one hundred families is pure joy. You have close, informal contact with your people. You can be one with and part of them."

What are the challenges of the rural parish's sense of the Church as "us?" First, because rural parishioners do not and will not go elsewhere for church activities, especially worship, rural parishes are extremely dependent on their pastors for a sense of a church beyond them, an understanding of Church direction and mission and emphasis. For the diocese, the implications of this reality demand limited tenure of pastors for the benefit of both clergy and the communities. A regular alternation of the gifts and talents and education that pastors and parishes offer to each other is a vital gift to the rural parish. I know of several rural parishes who lived for ten or fifteen years as though the Second Vatican Council had never happened because, as far as their pastors were concerned, it had never happened. That is simply unjust.

Dioceses need special sensitivity to the rural parish in the face of the declining number of priests. At the least, the term "mission" should be eliminated from popular ecclesiastical terminology. In the past a "mission" became a "parish" as the community grew. Today, the new "mission" means decline is on the way. At the most, dioceses must foster the development of a variety of team ministries. In my diocese, three parishes, each with a priest administrator, are beginning to work together on educational activities. Each of the priests presides at the Sunday Eucharist at each of the parishes. In another situation, four parishes are joining together in a similar fashion. They have established a four-parish board in addition to their parish councils. Together they have hired a pastoral minister for the new four-parish ministry. In areas with fewer priests, former parishes have been combined to form one new parish; the work in these situations is to establish a common identity while maintaining the individual spirit of the original parishes.

The overriding challenge to diocesan and local ministers is the development of ministers and ministries in the rural parish — to tap adult education resources at deanery, regional, and diocesan levels; to encourage, call forth, and develop the gifts of the people for the strengthening of the parish. This can only strengthen the competence of each rural community and link them to the network and vision of the diocesan church. This will build a bridge between the rural parish distinction between the Church as "us" and the Church as "them."

II. Rural Parishes and Liturgy

There are three essential tools which persons who are responsible for overseeing the liturgical life of any parish community must have at their disposal. The difficulty with these tools is that, of course, they take work and commitment on the part of the liturgist. But they are tools, not only for the one who is chiefly responsible for the liturgical life, but tools which must be used by whatever committees or groups share the responsibility for parish worship, ultimately the entire parish.

The three tools are: first, one's personal prayer, both private and liturgical; second, the patterns of prayer of the universal Church — in other words, the liturgical tradition; and third, the prayer traditions of the community to which the liturgist is responsible.

1. Personal Prayer Patterns

The most powerful, formative resource for my ministry as a parish liturgist has been my own experience of faith and my faith experience at prayer, alone and in the liturgy. This is the most valuable workbook that any of us has. Turning our own experience of prayer into a tool for preparing liturgy requires more than the general awareness that "I pray" and "I believe." It requires the active recollection of our "prayer times" and the recording of them. It means that we delve into our own experiences and draw the structure out of them. We discover what it was about that retreat, that moment in the mountains, that baptism, that took hold of us and turned us inside out in readiness for the grace of God. Then it is available to us and we can assist a community to do the same.

It is possible in many communities to uncover a situation as the following. While I was working with a parish liturgy committee to prepare for the Advent and Christmas seasons, I asked the committee to recall past Christmas liturgies. One of our members told about a childhood Christmas when an ice storm had downed the power lines and most of the city went without electricity for half the day. But the experience of Christmas morning Mass was more memorable than the inconvenience of finding a gas stove to cook the Christmas turkey in. "Every candle in the church was brought out for Mass, the funeral candles, the vigil lights, the benediction candles. Every bit of available wax with a wick was lit. Every Christmas I think about that. It was the most wonderful and beautiful thing I have ever seen. It was far more moving than the electric lights on the evergreen trees." As the committee listened and began to look to the season's Scripture readings, we took note of the several references to Christ the light, the light for all nations, the light that shines in the darkness. One person's Christmas-past became the building block of a Christmas-present. And that Christmas was the beginning of a parish tradition.

The point of developing our own workbook of prayer memories is not to recreate the experience for ourselves or others. In the first place, it is impossible; in the second, it would be extremely narcissistic. Our experience is not the norm for others, but unless we consciously tend to our past prayer experience, a wealth of insight is lost. Awareness of our graced moments can provide occasions of grace for our community at prayer.

2. Liturgical Patterns

The second tool for pastoral liturgists is the liturgical tradition of the Church. The sacraments, the liturgical seasons and calendar, the rhythm of the week, and the place of Sunday are not separate items to be dealt with as time deals them out to us. Rather, they are components in an interdependent, interwoven system in which every part affects the whole. "Sacramental economy" is the phrase used to describe the balance and relatedness of the liturgical patterns of the Church. Within the rites themselves, the alternations between word and sacrament, proclamation and response, song and silence are a second tier of carefully interwoven dynamics with their own logic. The entire liturgical pattern is the accumulated wisdom of the prayer and insight of the generations of the Church. Parish liturgists act in ignorance if they act without understanding and respecting this heritage.

Personal insight, faith, and prayer alone are not enough for the parish liturgist. Most parish liturgy committee members offer their time with a great deal of hesitance because they have little academic knowledge of the liturgical tradition. However, they do bring a wealth of life and a history of praying the liturgy: that is why both the personal and the liturgical insights must be tapped and why the liturgist must provide the resources, training, and education in both these areas for the parishioners.

In the rural parish, the awareness of the natural rhythm of the seasons, of day and night, of life, death, and rebirth is much deeper than it is in city dwellers. While cultural change is absorbed more slowly in the country than in the city, the opportunity for the restoration and renewal of the liturgical economy is greater for liturgists who minister in a rural parish.

Many rural communities celebrate the Eucharist only once on Sunday. This is a blessing when it comes to celebrating the Easter Vigil as *the* Eucharist of the entire year. In a small, stable faith community which is highly conscious of spring rebirth, there is a strong sense of the natural rightness of "saving" all baptisms of children and adults for the Easter Vigil or at least the Easter season. Moreover, because farm work is often regulated less by electricity than by natural light, it may be more possible to initiate the Liturgy of the Hours, especially evening prayer. The groundwork for establishing these practices is done in a community whose work is dominated by the changing seasons.

If my experience of rural communities is an indication of the condition of liturgical education in rural parishes around the country, there is widespread ignorance of the liturgical tradition and the reasons for its current revision. While ignorance of liturgy is not peculiar to rural communities, it is more of an injustice to them than to city parishes. Rural people do not shop around for the best liturgy or have ready access to any number of parish Mass schedules to suit their weekend convenience. Rural parishes have less exposure to the possibilities of the liturgy beyond their own Sunday fare.

A minister who does not provide liturgical information to the rural parish does that parish a grave disservice. At one parish, which I visited at the pastor's request, I found worship committee members who were astounded to learn that they could touch the lectionary or that it contained anything that might be of use to them apart from the Scripture lessons. At another parish, the liturgy committee begged me for resources. "If you know these things, what can we read that will help us to know what we should be doing?"

Explaining and establishing good patterns of worship is a primary goal for any parish. Beyond that, it is necessary to share liturgical sources, to give the parishioners the tools to work with, no matter what the luck of the above-mentioned lottery provides. I have heard people complain too often that the present pastor will not allow what the pastor before him encouraged, and vice versa. Most of the time, the regulation has only to do with nonessentials, but the people do not know that.

3. Local Patterns of Worship

These reflections lead naturally into a consideration of the particular parish's traditions. The community at hand is the community with which one does the liturgy. This may seem too obvious to note; however, too many ministers come to a new place of ministry with a carload of materials with which to bombard, reform, and remake a community into their own image of the kingdom. The community is new only to the new minister. It has usually been there long enough to establish its own traditions for good or for bad and, whether good or bad, these traditions deserve any minister's understanding. In rural parishes, particularly, a bulldozer approach will meet stubborn resistance. A change that is not perceived as being good for the community will be resisted because it threatens the community's stability. Rural people are not opposed to change *per se*; agricultural communities constantly adapt to new methods of farming, new chemicals, new equipment. When it is demonstrated that the change at hand is genuinely for the good of the community, the difficulty disappears.

The key problem for liturgists working with a community tradition is to distinguish between a "sacred cow" and something that is truly held sacred. This is particularly significant in a rural setting with a long and deeply rooted history. In general, a sacred cow is anything which receives no other response than "We've always done it that way before." I once saw a cartoon which suggested that those are the seven last words of Catholicism. Practices which fall in this category, if they are truly out of step with the mind of the Church, are areas for persistent, patient, and eventual change.

The sacred is less easily discerned. The following incident illustrates it well. A new pastor was assigned to a Mexican-American parish in rural Texas. Shortly after arriving, he remodeled the church according to the latest liturgical directives. He was quite responsible with the second tool we mentioned above—he respected and put into practice the best the liturgical tradition had to offer. But, with the renovation, the graphic larger-than-life crucifix went out the door, and the parishioners followed the crucifix. They took it from home to home for their own devotions. When the next pastor arrived, a delegation of parishioners was sent to ask him, "Will you accept our Jesus in your church?"

Our judgments must be based on more than our personal preferences; we must ask how a people's piety is formed and what provides continuity for their faith. To violate a community's sense of the sacred in the name of ours is effectively to create a stumbling block in the way of meeting the Lord.

The most obvious application of the principle of respect for the rural community's traditions concerns the seasonal work patterns of the community. The farmers' presentation of harvest gifts along with the bread and wine at the Eucharist with Pope John Paul II in Des Moines was more than a nice touch. In the suburban parish in which I worked, these gifts would have been merely a lovely autumn centerpiece. But for the people of the diocese of Des Moines, who were carrying up the results of their labor, those gifts represented their joy and their sweat—their lives. Is that not what the presentation of the gifts is about, bringing forth our lives for the thanksgiving and offering which is to follow? The blessing of seed and fields; prayer for good crops, good weather, and a bountiful harvest; responsible stewardship of the land—these are no small matters. People come to pray for the blessing of God on their work.

One of the mistakes that can be made by ministers who are not familiar with the farming schedule is to arrange programs and special events at periods of the year and hours of the day which interfere with the critical times of planting and harvesting. On the other hand, the rhythms of a local community's life, the ways in which they particularly seek the Lord's blessing, and the times when they are ready to celebrate are the sources of established traditions of prayer and also sources for starting new traditions of prayer.

During Pope John Paul's visit to St. Patrick's Parish in Irish Settlement, Iowa, he described their parish as "a small, unpretentious church at the center of a group of family farms, a place and a symbol of prayer and fellowship, the heart of a real Christian community where people know each other personally, share each other's problems, and give witness together to the love of Jesus Christ." He added, "Let your small community be a true place of Christian living and of evangelization, not isolating yourselves from the diocese or from the universal Church, knowing that a community with a human face must also reflect the face of Christ."

My bishop's motto is "Ecclesia agricultura" — the Church is a field to be harvested. And the harvest is rich.

The Alternative Parish Experience

DOLLY SOKOL AND JACK DOHERTY

In 1969, in a contribution to *Commonweal's* "Occasional Papers," Gregory Baum wrote:

> When we ask the question, where in fact the Catholic people are being inspired, instructed, nourished, and built up in Christ, we no longer point to the parish. It is rather a wide network of centers, chapels, discussion groups, lecture series, press columns, radio and television programs, worship centers in different places, private conversations and reading books that perform this ministry. . . . People no longer feel bound to the territorial parish, they elect their own style of being Catholic and, if present legislation of the Church interferes with plans they have for the future, they feel free to solve problems in their own way![1]

Eleven years later, in June 1980, we can still find much truth in those words. Still, I hope that our contribution to this year's Conference testifies to our fundamental disagreement with the statement that the parish can no longer be looked to for instruction, nourishment, and support. We are here today because we,

1. Gregory Baum, "Occasional Papers," *Commonweal* 91 (October 31, 1969) 127.

DOLLY SOKOL is a member of the ministerial team at the Ford City Catholic Center and is employed by the liturgy training program in Chicago.

JACK DOHERTY is a priest of the archdiocese of Chicago. He is currently a team member at the Ford City Catholic Center and has been responsible for worship in several Chicago parishes.

like many in our community, receive much of our nourishment from the parish community within which we worship.

This paper is divided into three parts. In the first, we shall offer some reflections on the theology — or, perhaps more accurately, on a spirituality — of parish, and then we shall give an account of the origins and development of the Ford City Catholic Center. In the second part, we shall share some of the aspects of our community's devotional and sacramental life. In the third and final section, we shall share some reflections on the strengths and weaknesses to be found in our style of alternative parish community.

I. A Spirituality of Parish

In preparing this paper, I went to my files to look for the folder marked "parish," only to find that, to my surprise, we did not have one. So much for being prepared. To help me clarify my thoughts on the subject, then, I begged and borrowed anything I could read on parish. What follows consists of some ideas about parish based on twelve years of pastoring set in dialogue with some of the research I did.

At root, "parish" is a Greek word meaning a camper or sojourner. The sojourner is a person, just like us, who dwells in a place as a temporary resident, as a stranger or alien. He or she is a traveler, a pilgrim. So are we all. We began our sojourn in this world as aliens, suffering the alienation we call "original sin." In the course of our sojourn on this earth, we are moving from alienation to communion — with ourselves, with our God, with others. Because of original sin, we can choose to remain alienated, even though we have been made heirs of our Father in baptism. We can tell ourselves terrible lies and remain cut off from the rhythms of our own lives, from our God, and from the call to enter into communion with others. But, through the graciousness of God, the Church now belongs to the definition of what it means to be human; as we move from alienation to communion, we now have a visible sign — the Church calling us to a process of humanization. For what does it mean to become fully human if not to engage in a process of moving from alienation to communion, from isolation to union with God and with his people?

It is thus the Church's mission to promote communion and communication. To speak of the Church is to speak of our "drawing together," of such redemptive structures as dialogue, healing, and evangelization. In their statement on parishes, the American bishops write: "The parish is the most powerful instrument the Church has to make itself known to men and women."[2] It is at the parish level that the Church touches people's lives right where they live. It is not without reason, then, that in the light of this redemptive, humanizing process of moving from alienation to communion, the Church should define itself again and again in familial and nurturing images. That, too, is why we as parishioners call out to each other for love, support, and communion. It is never easy to be a sojourner; it is hard to be on the road and to have no real home on this earth. For that reason, the Church has for the last thousand years used the structure of the parish, in all its many forms, to call out to the pilgrim and to let the sojourner know: We are beside you; we stand under you; as parish and community, we are one who serves.

Today, many feel, we are at a critical point in the history of the parish. I wonder if that is not healthy? To say, on the one hand, that we are family, community, and home for one another; and to say, on the other hand, that we are pilgrims and strangers and have no home on earth — this can only create tension within us and among us. Yet tension is not necessarily bad; it is what we see in tension and what we do with it that counts. I wonder, even after all these years since Vatican II, whether the tension we are experiencing today is telling us that we still do not

2. The full text appears in *The Parish: A People, A Mission, A Structure*, A Statement of the Committee on the Parish, National Conference of Catholic Bishops (Washington: United States Catholic Conference, 1980).

"have it together" where parish is concerned. Maybe if we looked at the root of our tension, we might find that God has called us once again into the solitude of the desert. Maybe in the hostile atmosphere of the desert, we can find out why so many parishes are suffering so much pain and unheaval. Maybe in the desert solitude, we will realize that the Church and the parishes, like all sojourners and travelers, cannot remain in the oasis forever. Today we are at a turning point: we can become nostalgic for Egypt — for the safe and ordered parish living of old — or we can travel onward into the desert, trusting as best we can that the pillar of fire, the abiding spirit of God's love, still hovers over our confusion and will make sense of our wandering. We can trust that it will lead us to the road of ongoing renewal, help us see new possibilities, dream new dreams, and discover the ancient truth that it is God, not we, who makes all things new.

Perhaps Henry Nouwen, in his book *Clowning in Rome*, hit the nail on the head when he wrote, "It is in solitude we indeed realize that community is *not* a common ideology, but a response to a common call. In solitude we realize that community is not made, but given."[3] Solitude is found in the desert. Whole parishes, as well as individuals, can be called to the desert. It may be that our wanderings — in our evaluations, programs of formation for ministry, and conferences — will bring us to see the Lord and to find the working models of parish and community that we seek.

II. FORD CITY CATHOLIC CENTER: ROOTS AND EVOLUTION

It was in the late 1960s, when Gregory Baum was writing about the demise of the parish, that the ideas of what we now know as the Ford City Catholic Center began to germinate. Other than

---

3. Henry Nouwen, *Clowning in Rome: Reflections on Solitude, Celibacy, Prayer and Contemplation* (Garden City, N.Y.: Image Books; Doubleday & Co., 1979) 13.

being a little more hopeful than now, the climate within the Church was much as it is today. It was the best of times, it was the worst of times.

There was no priests' senate in the church of Chicago in those days. There was, however, an Association of Chicago Priests. We came together, in the hope and enthusiasm engendered by Vatican II, to do battle with the structures of the church of Chicago and to dream dreams of renewal in ministry.

There was a new notion in the air at the time: that of "shared ministry" or "team ministry." The Association of Chicago Priests petitioned the Cardinal to establish team ministry in the church of Chicago. He agreed, with the consequence that two priests, three sisters, and a group of lay people came together to plan and to form themselves into a team. Sites and locations were investigated and presented to the Cardinal, but he chose instead an area on the southwest side of Chicago where an innercity shopping center and apartment complex were to be constructed. The area had been zoned as industrial, with the result that no existing parishes regarded it as being within their boundaries. The area was to be known as the Ford City Shopping Center because the existing buildings had at one time housed the Ford Motor Plant. The parish would be known as the Ford City Catholic Center.

If there were any parishioners who would be assigned to the Center simply for geographical reasons, it would be the residents of the Ford City Village Apartments; but the Ford City Catholic Center would essentially be an official, non-territorial, experimental parish of the church of Chicago. As *non-territorial*, it would be a parish of choice for people wherever they lived, regardless of whatever geographical parish they might come from. As *experimental*, Ford City would have a team of priests, sisters, and lay people who would be coresponsible as pastors to the community. Being experimental also meant that there would be no church building, no school. The sisters would rent one of the apartments, and the priests, without benefit of cook or housekeeper, would live in a bungalow just off the shopping center.[4] As *official*, the Catholic Center would not be a "floating parish." The only sense in which it could be said to be an "underground parish" was that the offices and worship space were to be located in the lower level, or basement, of the shopping center!

At first, few people came to Mass; but gradually, by word of mouth, news of the Catholic Center spread. Many who came were people looking to make church happen. Many, too, were people who had been away from the Church for a long time or had been hurt by traditional Church structures. No one, in those early days, really knew what direction to take. For the priests and sisters involved, all of whom had been trained to work independently, working as a team was a challenge. Nor was it only the team that had to make adjustments. As the Catholic Center was taking shape, so was the shopping center, with the result that we had repeatedly to move our celebrations of the Eucharist from one location to another, and people, on arriving, had to search around to find where we were gathering.

The starting point for adult formation was the liturgy planning meetings. Team and people met together in people's homes to reflect on the next weekend's readings. It was from the explanation of the Scriptures and the shared personal reflections that the intercessions, the choice of music, and the shape of the homily emerged.

A committee was formed to establish goals for the center, but through all the ups and downs of those years — perhaps *because* of them — the center evolved into the form it has today.

Today the Ford City Catholic Center is still in the basement of the shopping center, and about three hundred families call it their parish, their community. Today the team consists of two

---

4. When the original site in a northwestern suburban area was rejected by the Cardinal in 1969, the lay people who were originally to have been part of the team found that for personal, family, and economic reasons they were unable to make the transition to the south side. As a result, the team was without lay participation until the first laywoman joined in 1975, six years later.

diocesan priests, two permanent deacons, two sisters, and Dolly. Having done without a church building for so long, and having set the North Room up for Mass and then taken it down afterwards for every Sunday and holy day for eleven years, our liturgies are a combination of very sacred ingredients and very down-home elements. But we certainly know that we are church; we are aware of the right and duty of each person within the community to be a minister, to proclaim his or her piece of the Good News. Today we still have no grade school, and our community's educational thrust is still towards adults. (The weekend liturgies are still prepared at planning meetings, but these are now held once a month.) We have a religious education program at grammar school and high school levels, but the grammar school program is family-centered, to encourage parents and children to come together.

We have neither men's nor women's organizations in the traditional sense, though there is a women's group which looks at women's issues in contemporary society. We have offered a number of specific programs, the topics determined by the needs of the people and the skills of the staff. We have covered such matters as personality and growth, communications and journey; we have run a men's-only Scripture group, introduced the Genesis II program, and held a workshop on prayer for beginners. Still, if we measure our priorities in terms of budget allocation and energy spent, we are a Eucharist-centered community.

We regard everything we do as formative. Liturgy, lay involvement, and parish staffing are all viewed from this perspective, for we believe the Church consists of all who belong to it. The image we have of ourselves as Church is continually in process and continues to change as people and staff come and go. We regard ministry as a communal affair: the full-time professional and the ordinary parishioner alike are called to minister. Men and women—clergy, religious, and lay people— work as equals on the team. The original team and its original vision are both gone, but the center survives. The present community, with its pastoral team, continues to struggle and to succeed, to grapple and to fail, journeying together to form community.

Though different from the ordinary parish, and an alternative to it, the Ford City Catholic Center remains well within the thousand-year-old tradition of parish. Yet it is unique, and because it is unique it can offer a critique of much of what happens in the traditional parish. And we can also learn from the traditional parish. For this reason, given that we are at a critical turning point in the history of the parish structure, it would be foolish for us not to exchange experiences and learn from one another.

In the final section of this paper, we shall try to evaluate our community and see what that evaluation might have to teach us at the center and what it might have to offer the parishes. Yet there is one thing I discovered in doing research for this paper which strikes me as highly significant: nowhere in my reading of theological investigations and episcopal statements was there a suggestion that we ought to pray to the Lord for the gift of community. But, if community, like prayer, is a grace, how can we ever hope to attain it unless we not only work for it and search for it but also pray for it?

III. THE DEVOTIONAL AND SACRAMENTAL LIFE OF THE F.C.C.C.

To explore the devotional and sacramental life of the Ford City Catholic Center, we must first turn to the conciliar and postconciliar documents — in particular, the liturgy documents. From its inception, the pastoral staff and community has sought to put flesh on those documents, to make them alive and real in the celebrations of this faith community. At the same time, we have sought to create a spirit of hospitality in which the gift of community could be rooted and nurtured. Article 13 of the Instruction on Eucharistic Worship states: "No Christian community can be built up unless it has as its basis and pivot the celebration of the holy Eucharist. It is from this therefore that any attempt to form a community must begin." And the Constitution on the Sacred Liturgy (10) insists: "The liturgy is the summit towards which the activity of the Church is directed; it is also the fount from which all her power flows." The question of which comes first, the chicken or the egg, is also applicable here. This is very difficult, even in hindsight, to discern. They seem to have grown and been nurtured hand in hand. The community is formed through the Eucharist, and yet the Eucharist flows from the life of the community. This can be seen clearly when we first look at the history of liturgy planning meetings at the Catholic Center.

Eleven years ago, when the pastoral staff began its work of nurturing community, liturgy planning meetings played a significant part. Each Tuesday evening the pastoral staff would gather with community members to reflect on the Scriptures for the upcoming weekend. These meetings were open to all, with invitations extended in the bulletin, by announcement, and, most importantly, by personal invitation. The meeting would begin with prayer, followed by proclamation of the weekend's Scripture passages. Then the staff would share and invite others to share their reflections on the Scripture passages, on how they saw them enfleshed in their own lives. At first, the community members present looked to the priests for the correct interpretation of the Scriptures and for historical background. But once that was accomplished, and as various people began to know each other and trust themselves to one another, sharing would take place on a deeper level. The proclamation and interiorization of the word would lead to prayerful reflection, which might in turn lead to conversion and/or action. The meetings did much to make real article 24 of the Constitution on the Liturgy, which states: "Sacred scripture is of the greatest importance in the celebration of the liturgy. . . . it is essential to promote [a] warm and living love for scripture."

One of the significant aspects of the liturgy planning meetings, besides that of deep faith-sharing, was that the homily was formed right at the meeting. That is, the homilist for the upcoming weekend would take notes as the discussion progressed, and those notes would become the basis for his homily. The reflections, the thoughts, the faith-sharing, and the strength of each person was affirmed as they saw themselves significantly contributing to the development of the Sunday celebration. The Constitution on the Liturgy (35:2) instructs that the character of the sermon "should be that of a proclamation of God's wonderful works in the history of salvation, which is the mystery of Christ ever made present and active in us, especially in the celebration of the liturgy." The sermon was, indeed, that proclamation for our people, who witnessed their own lives take on deeper meaning as they listened to the homily on the following weekend. For the homilist spoke not only to them, but about them and with them.

But that was not the end of liturgy meetings. Once notes for the homily were taken, prayers formed, and music chosen, the staff and community shared a meal. Whether it was coffee and cake, cheese and crackers, homemade pizza, or diet pop and potato chips, almost everyone stayed around until well after the close of the formal part of the meeting to learn about each other, each other's family, friends, jobs, common interests, common visions, past parish experiences, and the like. Much of the conversation would flow directly from the sharing which took place at the meeting. No one was forced into speaking either during the meeting or afterwards, yet when each was ready, the invitation was always present to share with the community a part of themselves and to be accepted as who they were and where they were.

Another principle which formed the foundation of the Ford City Catholic Center's liturgical life is found in article 14 of the Constitution on the Liturgy: "In the restoration and promotion of the sacred liturgy, the full and active participation by all the people is the aim to be considered before all else." This was certainly characteristic of even the first Masses celebrated at the center and still continues to be a basic principle in our worship. All are encouraged and affirmed in their active participation. For, as the community took shape, we came to realize the primacy of our liturgical role as the assembly. We realized that we need each other at the Eucharist, we rely on each other at the Eucharist, and we have a responsibility to each other as baptized Christians at the Eucharist to be present in the fullest sense at the community meal.

One of the strongest signs of our attempt to embody this principle is the sign of music. From the beginning, music has been integral to our community celebration. It has been rooted in ministry rather than in performance. As article 23 of Music in Catholic Worship states:

> Music should assist the assembled believers to express and share the gift of faith that is within them and to nourish and strengthen their interior commitment of faith. It should heighten the texts so that they speak more fully and more effectively. The quality of joy and enthusiasm which music adds to community worship cannot be gained in any other way. It imparts a sense of unity to the congregation and sets the appropriate tone for a particular celebration.

And that it truly does. It is important to note that the music of the Catholic Center has always been in the folk idiom. Initially, many were attracted to Catholic Center liturgies for this reason alone. It was a folk Mass with guitars in an area of Chicago where most neighboring parishes and, in fact, many archdiocesan parishes abhorred the secularism of the music and instruments and refused to admit them into community worship. So people came expecting to be able to participate, and in fact they were strongly encouraged and helped to do so. Two additional aspects which added greatly to people's willingness to participate in this folk Mass were that the music was, and has been throughout the years, ministered by adults; and secondly, not by a folk group. Our ministers of music have consistently been competent adult musicians and people of faith who have been able to guide the community into expressing their faith in song as adults. We are lucky to have never fallen into the "this-liturgy-is-only-for-kids" trap. Also, participation was fostered in a significant way by not having a folk group, but instead only one or two people leading the assembly in song. This called the community to become active rather than passive listeners. No one was performing. Ministers of music led the community in song and prayer, counting on the support of one another to sustain this musical liturgy.

As might be supposed, the weekly liturgy planning meetings, together with the weekly celebration of the Eucharist, formed the beginnings of community. As people entered the Gold Room each weekend, they continued their life-sharing. Conversation, hospitality, and greeting were encouraged by staff members and followed through by the community. It was seldom that a newcomer was not greeted at the door, warmly welcomed, and invited to join in community worship. At coffee and conversation following the Sunday liturgy, plans were made between staff and community members and between community members themselves to meet and share with each other during the week outside the scheduled meetings of the community. A true sense of belonging began to take shape in this underground meeting room. People sensed that they no longer needed a building to be church—all they needed was a gathering of the People of God.

As the community grew in faith and in the Spirit, the giftedness of the people in the community was called forth by the pastoral staff and by one another. Community members were affirmed in their talents and called forth to minister. In the liturgy, women as well as men were from the start called forth to share their gifts as lectors, commentators, eucharistic ministers, and ministers of music.

As liturgy planning meetings continued and knowledge of liturgical principles increased in the community, a time came for the staff and community to face some important realities. The

Alternative Parish

liturgy of each Sunday is part of a liturgical year, and that year has cycles. While each weekend liturgy at the center seemed to be effective in itself, it was seldom that the liturgies were fitted together into liturgical seasons. The community, therefore, was not being led through the rhythms of the Christian liturgical year. The paschal mystery, while spoken of and celebrated in each liturgy, did not form the basis for community prayer throughout the year. It was from these feelings, and as a result of futile attempts to try to combine seasonal planning with weekly faith-sharing meetings, that the liturgy team evolved. The liturgy team was formed of community and staff members who were interested in delving deeper into the eucharistic liturgy and into the seasons that our Church celebrates throughout the year. Membership was open to anyone with those interests. Through the first year, the liturgy team concerned itself with a study of the Mass. Through prayer, reading, workshops, and discussion, members began to understand the traditions which have shaped our liturgy and the implications of the conciliar and postconciliar documents for those traditions. Many were surprised to see how our community had already put into practice so many of the norms given in the documents. From the prayerful deliberations of the liturgy team, in conjunction with the expertise of several staff members, changes in the manner of celebrating weekend liturgies were adopted in order to conform even more to the spirit of the Council. Following that initial year of education, the liturgy team explored the rhythm of the liturgical year and sought to give shape to the various seasons. This shape was then passed on to the liturgy planning meetings as they reflected on a particular weekend's Scripture.

The non-eucharistic sacramental life of the community is also guided by the Council. In the Constitution on the Liturgy (27), we read:

> It is to be stressed that whenever rites make provision for communal celebration involving the presence and active participation of the faithful, this way of celebrating them is to be preferred so

far as possible to a celebration that is individual and quasi-private.

And so we celebrate baptisms as a community at Sunday Eucharist, affirming our own baptisms in Christ and welcoming the child through his or her entire family into the Christian community of faith. Anointing, too, is celebrated communally once a year with our many parishioners who are elderly or feel themselves in need of healing. The entire community is called upon to manifest their care and concern for the sick and elderly of our parish by helping with transportation, by visiting, by baking for the celebration after Mass. Doctors and nurses from the community are present in uniform and assist in any way possible. Reconciliation, too, is celebrated communally during the seasons of Advent and Lent. We have no confessionals. Those who seek to celebrate the sacrament individually are asked to call and make an appointment with one of the priests directly. Confirmation of our juniors and seniors in high school is celebrated every other year as a community event. Marriages and funerals do take place, but because of our location, we "borrow" a church building in the neighborhood in which to celebrate the occasion.

Article 59 of the Constitution on the Liturgy teaches that "the purpose of the sacraments is to sanctify, to build up the body of Christ, to give worship to God." It states clearly that the sacraments "not only presuppose faith, but . . . they also nourish, strengthen, and express it." And that is what we try to achieve in our sacramental celebrations.

Communal devotional life is linked exclusively to liturgical prayer. Mass is not celebrated daily, but we do celebrate Mass in the rectory basement on Tuesday evenings. We celebrate a special children's Liturgy of the Word weekly at our 10:45 a.m. Mass on Sunday; we celebrate the Liturgy of the Hours monthly; we celebrate the first Friday of the month with a Mass and social. We also celebrate a special Mass at 4:00 p.m. each Friday in the Ford City Village Apartments for our shut-ins and senior citizens. Since we have always made weekly Communion calls to our shut-ins, the Friday afternoon Mass, which celebrates the liturgy of the upcoming weekend, was initiated with two purposes in mind. First, it would naturally lessen our weekly Communion calls because most would be able to use the elevators in the high-rise building and come to the Mass celebrated in the apartment of one of the shut-ins. Second—and perhaps more important—the gathering of these people at the high-rise Mass began to create and nurture community among these otherwise isolated and lonely people. The constant care which they now offer to one another testifies to the success of this experience.

However, all these experiences of liturgical prayer in our community do not imply that we have no personal devotional life. As the Constitution on the Liturgy states in article 9: "The sacred liturgy does not exhaust the entire activity of the Church. Before [people] can come to liturgy they must be called to faith and conversion." We seek to live out this principle, this call to continual conversion and deepening of faith, through our personal prayer and spiritual formation. For most of the eleven years of the community's existence, two retreats have been offered in a desert-like place. These retreats encourage both community formation and personal spiritual formation. Retreat teams are made up of both staff and community members. Personal spirituality has also been developed through workshops in communication skills given by staff members. Over the years, several members of the staff have always been specifically trained in spiritual direction, so community members have been able to find nourishment for their spiritual development through this kind of guidance as well. A program which has also been welcomed in the last two years is a prayer-for-beginners program based on the book *You: Prayer for Beginners and Those Who Have Forgotten How* by Mark Link, S.J. Community members have discovered the need to find a time and place for daily private prayer, and they have responded to it.

Since we have no church building, it is even more incumbent upon us to set aside a portion of our home as a prayer place and to go to it daily to put ourselves into dialogue with the Holy One. This year, as part of our keeping of Lent, all community members were invited to keep a journal of their Lenten reflections. They were given journal sheets each weekend with several questions to direct their reflection. They were invited to go to prayer openhanded — to open their clenched fists, to see what in their lives needed to be surrendered in order to live a more fully Christian life — and so they were invited to enter into the process of death and resurrection within themselves. Also, this year, a program called "At Home Retreats" was initiated — a thirteen-week program based on the Spiritual Exercises of St. Ignatius of Loyola, offered to married men and women in the community. A team composed of both staff and community members took instruction in this method and offered the retreat experience. In addition, the ministry of *Laudator* has recently been initiated. People are asked to serve the community by praying for five minutes a day for the needs of the community. Again, many senior citizens are drawn into this ministry and are affirmed as serving the community in a very real and significant way.

In both the sacramental and the devotional life of the community, parishioners of the Ford City Catholic Center seek to enflesh the spirit of Jesus Christ and then to live out that baptismal commitment in our lives with our families, our community, our neighborhood, our place of employment, our world. We strive to remain faithful to that directive of the Council which states, in article 9 of the Constitution on the Liturgy:

> The Church announces the Good News of salvation to those who do not believe, so that people may know the true God and Jesus Christ whom he has sent. . . . To believers the Church must also preach faith and penance . . . and invite them to all the works of charity, piety and the apostolate. For these works make it clear that Christ's faithful, though not of this world, are to be the light of the world.

IV. Strengths and Weaknesses of the Alternative Parish

We have already touched upon some of the strengths and weaknesses of our Christian community life at the Ford City Catholic Center, but in this final section of the paper we would like to offer some more specific evaluations and reflections. There is, of course, some truth to the old cliché that every weakness is a strength and vice versa. To a large degree, such evaluations depend upon the criteria used by those making the judgment. For this reason, to escape the invidious task of passing judgment on our own labors, we polled the rest of the pastoral team and invited parishioners to fill out a questionnaire. From the responses we received, four broad areas emerged: parish size; parish administration; parishioner involvement; liturgy and spirituality. Clearly, these are areas of concern to all parishes, which encourages us to hope that the evaluation of our own experiences at Ford City might be of assistance to others.

1. Parish Size

Our community is small, roughly 250 to 300 families, plus a few shoppers who drop in on Saturdays. The constituency is basically lower middle class. We have attracted a large group of senior citizens, largely because of the proximity of the apartments on the shopping center property and the shuttle bus which runs between the apartments and the stores. There is a large percentage of families with children of high school or college age, a number of single adults, and a growing number of persons who are divorced or separated. Most have heard of us by word of mouth or through announcements about Mass which they heard while shopping. They have liked what they have experienced, and they have stayed. In our concern to publicize our presence, we have also had articles about us run in the *National Catholic Reporter (NCR), St. Anthony's Messenger*, the Chicago press, both religious and secular, and local community newspapers. Many of our people come from neighboring parishes and from the suburbs just south of us. Many who have since moved out of the area continue to come back each Sunday or even during the week for special programs, some traveling twenty or thirty miles to be with us.

It is the smallness of the community and the enthusiasm of our parishioners and staff which prompted replies such as the following to our question about why people come: "Warm community, sharing and supportive. It is easier to know and be known." On the debit side of the ledger, respondents also warned: "There is a great danger of becoming too introspective and of not broadening our horizons to stretch beyond ourselves. Fewer people to share ministries increases the risk of burn-out. Sometimes there is a feeling of lack of space and privacy. Sometimes we fall over each other to minister to each other. Misunderstandings cannot be hidden." When I came to the center from a parish of 3,000 families to one of 250, it seemed like heaven. In many ways, it still seems that way. Yet it remains true that the same amount of work often has to be done for six people as would need to be done for sixty or six hundred. In our present situation, with the shortage of priests, there is terrible uneasiness every time a priest is transferred: "Will we get a replacement? Will anyone want to come to such a place?" But those very same worries have forced our people to realize that the Ford City Catholic Center is their community. Clergy and religious come and go, but the people stay. Our people now say it — and live it and believe it — it is they and not we who are the core of the Ford City Catholic Center; and that is good. What this all means, though, is that people are dying to know that, when they worship before God or in community, they are not anonymous.

2. Parish Administration and Team Ministry

Parish administration is another area of our community life which has both its strengths and its weaknesses. The Catholic Center is administered by a team of seven co-pastors, consisting of two sisters, two permanent deacons, two priests, and a laywoman. Responsibility for various parish programs is likewise shared among the team members.

There are many strengths to this model of administration. First, team ministry itself bears witness that equality in ministry among clergy, religious, and laity is both possible and desirable. Second, because all team members share in the administration and decision-making for the community, we are all aware of what is going on in the community and are therefore more committed to and more supportive of both the programs and of one another. Third, team ministry allows for the more onerous duties of ministry—such as setting up the North Room or last-minute stuffing of bulletins—to be shared among us all. Fourth, teams made up of both male and female members give expression to the complementarity of the sexes and the totality of humankind; and fifth, the presence of lay members in team ministry gives perspective and support for the call of all people to ministry.

Regarding the team itself, we provide a good support system for one another. We relate to one another not only professionally, but personally. We strive to affirm as well as to confront and challenge one another; we try to develop and sustain genuine respect for one another's gifts and opinions, even in situations of conflict.

On the other hand, the administration and the development of team ministry are not without their difficulties. An obvious disadvantage of having administration in the hands of a team is that it naturally takes longer to come to a decision because a proposal has to go through a group-discussion process, rather than having one person make the final decision. However, outweighing this, we feel that the decisions reached are qualitatively better for the team and the community because they have been filtered through the experience and expertise of seven people. Moreover, besides being accountable to one another, team members are also directly accountable to the whole community at the Lay Involvement Meeting, a structure which we shall discuss in the next section.

Another difficulty in the formation and working of a team ministry is the process of shared decision-making itself. Such a process requires team members to possess some important interpersonal skills: skills in handling conflict and tension; skills in confronting and challenging; clarifying skills which permit team members to express themselves honestly in an atmosphere of trust. These skills are not always present, so feelings have sometimes to be worked through before the issue at hand can be addressed.

Changes in team membership are always difficult. As old members leave and new ones arrive, the team takes on a new shape, and the interpersonal skills and relationships must once again be cultivated. It is also important to recognize that not everyone is interested in or suited for team ministry. Many of us know good people who would be unable to function effectively in such a context. Because of this, we have developed a three-stage interview process for prospective team members: first the candidate is interviewed and evaluated by the person he or she will live with, then by the pastoral team, and finally by the community at large at a Lay Involvement Meeting. While the procedure is by no means perfect, it does give us an indication of a candidate's ability to live and work with the team and the community.

3. Parishioner Involvement and Ministry

When people hear about the Catholic Center, they often jump to the conclusion that we must have been one of the first parishes to have a parish council. It must be admitted that that is not true; even today we have no parish council. What we do have is a Lay Involvement Meeting. On the third Sunday of most months, the parish team meets with all those in the community who wish to attend. One of the team members is responsible for liaison with lay involvement; this person meets, two weeks before the meeting, with a parishioner who has volunteered to chair the meeting. They discuss the five areas that form the agenda for every Lay Involvement Meeting:

1. *Reports.* These cover the activities of the staff over the past month, usually by means of a summary of the minutes of the weekly two-hour staff meeting; financial report; and special reports on projects in progress, such as religious education or the "At-Home Retreat Group."

2. *Community Feedback.* This covers areas on which the staff would like some evaluation or more ideas, or looks for some consensus from the meeting.

3. *Additional Agenda.* This is mainly for follow-up questions on the reports presented.

4. *Date of Next Meeting* and volunteer to take the chair.

5. *Open Forum.* Here we consider any proposals that people want to make, any new ideas or concerns they would like to voice. It is an opportunity for community members to make their ideas known both to the staff and to the rest of the community.

It is by the people's choice that this lay involvement process has not evolved into a parish council. They have never wanted the involvement to be limited to those holding positions of responsibility within the community. It remains true that final decisions always rest with the team, but it would be only after much serious consideration that the staff would go against the wishes of the Lay Involvement Meeting. In fact, there is mutual trust: they trust us as a team; we trust the wisdom of the community.

In the responses to the questionnaire, the strengths and weaknesses of this structure were evaluated, and the findings were overwhelmingly positive. People find that it gives everyone a chance to lead at some times and to follow at others, so everyone has a chance to grow. They appreciate the meeting as a real study in how participatory democracy can work — and also as a study in group dynamics! The existence of the Lay Involvement Meeting is seen as evidence of the psychological health of the community and as symbolic of the collaboration which prevails in all areas of community life, preventing a "them-and-us" polarization. The laity have a real say — and *know* they have a real say — in community affairs, with the power to shape their community life.

4. Liturgy and Spirituality

Almost all the responses to our questionnaire saw the area of liturgy and spirituality as one of the overwhelming strengths of our community. Typical of the replies we received are the following:

- excellent, well-planned, and beautiful liturgies;
- continuity excellent in seasonal themes, music, and homilies;
- liturgies meet people where they are and then encourage growth;
- liturgies have an honest feeling to them, which comes from everyone giving input;
- creative liturgies, open to ever better celebration, but not open to fads;
- good homilies, good current liturgical music;
- inclusion of women in all possible areas of liturgical ministry;
- liturgies are evaluated regularly.

Several weaknesses were cited, and we have a few negative observations of our own to add.

It seems that there is a danger that liturgical and spiritual development can become ends in themselves, instead of means to an end. We need to continually present to our community and ourselves our mission, our call to be light for the world — to work to bring about the kingdom. And so we as a community need to become even more involved in issues of justice and to bring those concerns to the Lord and to one another at the Eucharist. We have made some positive steps in this direction in recent years. In 1977 the issue of racial justice became real for us, as mandatory bussing to achieve racial integration was called for in the Chicago Public Schools. The Bogan area, an all white neighborhood on Chicago's southwest side, was the scene of the most heated controversy. Ford City Catholic Center is located in the Bogan area. At that time, we, as a pastoral staff, tried to witness to the gospel message through our homilies, through our visible presence in front of the schools to which black children were being bussed, and through a pastoral letter. The letter, which was inserted in our bulletin on the first weekend after school began, was also sent to local and national newspapers, religious as well as secular. We were pleased to see that the *Southtown Economist* and the *Southwest News-Herald*, two local papers, as well as the *NCR*, printed the entire text of our letter. The *Chicago Sun-Times* also followed through with an article about our community. The publicity, of course, was not the end in itself. However, it did serve to speak to the wider community of its fears and yet challenge them to the growth called for in the gospel.

Another similar situation in terms of racial justice occurred the following summer. The American Nazi Party, headquartered in Marquette Park, just to the east of us, planned a march for white supremacy in Marquette Park. Having been denied a permit to march there, they somehow succeeded in obtaining a permit to march in Skokie, a suburb of Chicago which has the largest population of the Nazi Holocaust survivors in the United States. Again we, as a pastoral staff, felt compelled to lead a response. Three of our staff drove to Skokie to participate in an inter-denominational prayer service on the morning of the march and brought back petitions which we presented to our community for signature.

Also, during the weeks of ordinary time, we have tried to speak to the alienated, the divorced, the widowed, the married, and the single as we reflected on the Scriptures of those weekends. However, even with those efforts, we still feel that there is much more that we, as a staff and as a community, can do in light of our mission.

Another weakness in terms of liturgy is that we cannot use our own worship space at two of the peak liturgical moments in the lives of our parishioners, namely, weddings and funerals. In "borrowing" even the environmentally best church building in the area, we are still basically fish out of water and have difficulty creating the same spirit of hospitality in a strange space.

Aesthetically, while we do the best we can with the North Room, it really cannot inspire. Its architecture is not uplifting; there are no stained glass windows, no icons or statuary, no really empty space. Incense cannot really rise, processions cannot really process. The distance and depth which are conducive to some ritual actions are not present, so we cannot use those modes of expression. We also tend to suffer from paschal paranoia each Easter Vigil as we try to kindle the new fire without setting off the sprinkler system in the shopping center.

Another weakness in liturgy is to be found in the area of liturgical music. While excellent liturgical music is used each week, it is only in the folk idiom. Our community is not sharing in the growth of contemporary church music in other genres, and we seldom experience the wealth of traditional church music. Our people have no opportunity to experience the music of Peloquin, Isele, Proulx, Hughes, Hytrek, nor an organ prelude from Bach, nor the rich hymnody of past generations.

So, while the comments about our liturgical life as a community are most positive, the challenge is not to stagnate, but to strive continually to put ourselves in touch with our life experiences and then find ritual expression for those experiences.

We have described the community life and worship of the Ford City Catholic Center in Chicago. We have attempted to evaluate its strengths and weaknesses. In all this, we have attempted to show what "the alternative parish experience" has to offer. It is true that in many respects our story is unique, yet in other and more important ways we find ourselves sharing with our fellow believers in other parishes the Catholic story as it unfolds in our own time.

1980 MICHAEL MATHIS AWARD

TO MSGR. MARTIN HELLRIEGEL

Liturgical Pioneers and Parish Worship

A Response on the Occasion of the Michael Mathis Award to Monsignor Martin Hellriegel by the Notre Dame Center for Pastoral Liturgy, 1980

FREDERICK R. MCMANUS

It always strikes me as somewhat narcissistic to quote oneself, but I will venture it. Five years ago, in a newspaper piece, I listed the "American Liturgical Pioneers" and their accomplishments. The pioneers were Virgil Michel, Godfrey Diekmann, Hans Reinhold, Gerald Ellard, and Maurice Lavanoux. I added:

> No listing of pioneers would be complete without reference to the very many parish priests and lay leaders who translated

---

FREDERICK MCMANUS is an associate editor of *Worship* and director of the Secretariat, Bishops' Committee on the Liturgy, Washington, D.C. He is vice provost of The Catholic University of America and dean of the Graduate School; he is professor of canon law in the School of Religious Studies.

Since age and sickness prevented Martin Hellriegel from traveling to Notre Dame for the award, the presentation was actually made in St. Louis before the Conference at Notre Dame. Frederick McManus graciously agreed to deliver the customary acceptance address for his friend and mentor. Msgr. Hellriegel died a few months later, April 10, 1981.

pastoral theories into practice. One who may stand for all the rest is Msgr. Martin Hellriegel of St. Louis, now pastor emeritus of Holy Cross parish in that city. A towering and impressive figure of great faith and enthusiasm, Hellriegel has been known less for his writings than for his pastoral sense and ingenuity. With strong folk piety from his native Germany, he approached every parish celebration with warmth. His influence spread through his major role at the Liturgical Weeks, his translation of German hymns, his example of parish liturgy — even in the unreformed Latin — at its best.[1]

These words perhaps did not do justice to Martin Hellriegel's writings, and we will return to his success with even an unreformed liturgy in Latin. But the words reflect my deep personal esteem for Monsignor Hellriegel — long, long before I was flattered with the invitation to present a response for him on this occasion.

It is difficult to realize that few of those present here this morning were alive when Martin Hellriegel joined Gerald Ellard and Virgil Michel in 1925 as the original triumvirate, when Michel took the solemn decision to publish *Orate Fratres*, now *Worship*. Or that most present here were hardly seasoned liturgical promoters when Hellriegel became president of the Liturgical Conference in 1950 or even in 1956 when he came to Notre Dame for a pastoral symposium on the reformed Holy Week. I mention that symposium, sponsored by Fr. Michael Mathis, in whose memory today's award is given, because it was the first occasion when I had the honor to share a platform with Martin Hellriegel: he was being pastoral, I was being canonical. Mentioning our first joint appearance also gives me the opportunity to assure you and myself that I am not one of the liturgical pioneers referred to in the title of these remarks; in fact, I am thirty-three years younger, at least chronologically, than Martin Hellriegel.

---

1. "American Liturgical Pioneers," *Catholics in America,* ed. Robert Trisco (Washington: National Conference of Catholic Bishops, 1976) 157.

More seriously, the Notre Dame Center for Pastoral Liturgy honors itself in honoring Monsignor Hellriegel, partly for his own personal achievements—parochial, diocesan, and national —partly for the value of his work and style as models for today.

The few pioneers I have named very selectively may be quickly characterized. Virgil Michel, the founder of *Worship*, was indeed the founder of the American liturgical movement— and the one who set it on its sure course of social concern integrated with liturgical celebration; he was a scholar, writer, publicist, catechist, and mover. Godfrey Diekmann, who must have been a child monk—so long has been his distinguished career as Michel's continuator—is a teacher, preacher, writer, and, above all—and even today in his seventies—youthful enthusiast. Gerald Ellard was the Jesuit scholar and textbook writer who translated his scholarship into effective, eloquent books and articles far ahead of the times. Hans Reinhold, although pastor of a small parish, was best and correctly known for his wise, vivid, forceful, even caustic writings—in a sense unlike his simple and humble self. Maurice Lavanoux, tireless editor of *Liturgical Arts*, stands for the others who sought to integrate artistic forms with holy function; he was largely unhonored, although I am glad both Notre Dame University and The Catholic University gave him honorary degrees.

Others could be listed: Reinhold Hillenbrand, whose recent death we mourn, grasped and imparted the social and ecclesial implications of the liturgical apostolate; William Leonard and Aloysius Wilmes, Damasus Winzen and Michael Ducey: it is sad not to be able to give a moment to these and many others.

Among these great names, Martin Hellriegel was an extensive writer and publicist, but best known for his imaginative pastoral practice, for being a master teacher, for liturgical celebrations at the motherhouse of the Sisters of the Most Precious Blood in O'Fallon for twenty-two years and at Holy Cross Parish in St. Louis from 1940 to the present. The people who visited O'Fallon and Holy Cross, those with whom he corresponded, those who heard him at Liturgical Week after Liturgical Week, those who read his descriptions of parish worship in *Orate Fratres*, in books, in articles, in proceedings of The Liturgical Conference — all were moved and in some way shaped by his spiritual depth, pastoral sense, and gentle enthusiasm.

My brief, however, is not to tell the story of the liturgical pioneers, but to suggest some implications, themes, models, or lessons that may be as promising today as in the 1920s to the 1950s. In the case of Hellriegel, we are fortunate to have a dissertation-study of his work by Mrs. Noel H. Barrett, done at St. Louis University in 1976.[2] The breadth of the Hellriegel bibliography indicates that it would be worthwhile today to recapture some feeling for the efforts made and the rationale proposed for the liturgical apostolate of three or four decades back. The references to an unreformed Roman liturgy are dated, and the ecclesial and social circumstances are so changed that I would hardly propose a reading of volumes of *Orate Fratres* from cover to cover. But it would be instructive to read through the articles for a given year or, more thematically, to read a volume or two of the Liturgical Week proceedings which began in 1940 — on liturgy and social order, on Christian initiation, on Church unity, and so on. If there are lessons to be learned — and I think there are — it is necessary to recapture a sense of the situation and context in which the pioneers flourished.

It is tempting, of course, in the tone of a *laudator temporis acti*, to describe in Hellriegel or in other pioneers attitudes and approaches which much later, in the sixties and seventies, seemed newly discovered. We now are concerned with the style of celebration and body language, especially of those who preside. Of Hellriegel in the early forties it was said: "He did things around the altar like they were the most important things in the world. . . . you'll get the sensation that when he says

---

2. Noel H. Barrett, *The Contribution of Martin B. Hellriegel to the American Catholic Liturgical Movement* (St. Louis: Saint Louis University, 1976).

Gloria in excelsis Deo he's saying it with all the enthusiasm and wonderment of a person proclaiming the words for the first time." Today we theorize about the parish community and sub-communities and theologize about it all. In 1940 Hellriegel consciously approached the pastoral office with the philosophy that "the parish itself . . . should be the primary society or organization, taking precedence over any societies or organizations within the parish. The Eucharist should be the primary parish activity, having priority over any other parish function. Next in significance as a center of parish activities should be the family; the life of the parish should strengthen family ties rather than put demands on the members of the family that pull them away from one another."

It is equally tempting to give examples of specific usages, of signs and symbols, that Hellriegel used creatively to bring the Church year and its rhythms to life. More broadly, our current concerns for liturgical catechesis prior to liturgical change and for celebration working as it were from the inside out, from inner piety to outward articulation, all were anticipated and treated as normal expectations in the pioneering work of the preconciliar decades.

Again, it is not my brief to seek out evidence to demonstrate the insights or the foresights of pioneers that long anticipated our concerns for vital parish worship. Rather, it is to propose for reflection some lessons for contemporary worship from the work and words of the pioneers.

First, I would point out how much effort went into the theoretical study of the liturgy in the decades before the Second Vatican Council, the effort to understand biblically, theologically, historically, spiritually, and ritually the celebration of the Church, its sacramental nature, the integration of Eucharist and life. Admittedly, the pastors, writers, leaders, and those who listened were the smallest fraction of the body of priests and educated laity of that day, but their involvement was theoretically well based, the fruit of serious, if not scholarly, study.

Today those who are involved and trying hard are vastly larger in numbers and in proportion. I daresay they include a considerable majority of those who hold the pastoral office or who help to shape our parish liturgies: the priests, the committees, the leaders. I fear, however, that our theoretical study and knowledge have not been pursued in proportion to the need, especially the need created by the relative freedom to innovate and invent in the reformed liturgy. To put it another way, the written literature of today seems to be too much pragmatic and how-to-do-it, sometimes superficial, often endless examples of liturgies with little theoretical base.

A moment ago I suggested that we should dip into the writings of the pioneers to appreciate the liturgical situation in which they worked, at a time when, for example, it was unheard of that people should share in eucharistic Communion at a funeral Mass. Now I suggest that a study of such writings—especially, I think, the proceedings of Liturgical Weeks—will demonstrate a deep interest in theory and even scholarship, including, of course, much derivative scholarship. Participants in the Liturgical Weeks of the forties and fifties were pragmatic and certainly pastoral in their interests, but they recognized the need for theory, doctrine, history, study.

Today the numbers of those who "do" the liturgy have increased many times over—in the sense of those who prepare, plan, and develop liturgies, over and above those who preside over them. But perhaps we have not been sufficiently eager to explore and to study.

What I have been saying bears an obvious relationship to the liturgical preparation of ordained ministers, a preparation which seems to be little better than that of several decades back. We can applaud at least the intentions of the recent document on liturgical formation in seminaries, commented upon by Thomas Krosnicki and John Gurrieri in *Worship*.[3] And whatever our

3. Thomas A. Krosnicki and John A. Gurrieri, "Seminary Liturgy Revisited," *Worship* 54 (1980) 158–169.

judgment about the new Roman instruction on eucharistic aberrations, at least we can welcome its call for liturgical formation. My point is that, like the pioneers, we must devote more time and energy to the theoretical, whether spiritual or theological or ritual.

There are bright signs in the kinds of study material issued by some commissions, diocesan and national. The popular success of Aidan Kavanagh's excellent book on initiation is another instance, followed now by the new volume by Richard Rutherford on funerals; and at a moment when we may be on the defensive in such matters, the works of Thomas Richstatter and, more recently, Kevin Seasoltz on liturgical discipline provide some theory to support our pastoral and parish practice.[4] I submit that we need an exhaustive study—a kind of combined Jungmann, Dix, and Parsch for the eighties—of the Order of Mass, the Order of eucharistic celebration. Negatively, this is needed so that our practical creativity does not go astray; positively, it is needed to open up both the sense of the Order and its rich opportunities still unexplored.

Today we can learn from our pioneer models the critical need for sound underpinnings of practice. To put it plainly and as example, every doctrinal or theoretical sentence of the general instruction of the Roman Missal should be studied exhaustively by all who share responsibility for parish worship.

These references to the Eucharist bring me to my second point. From his ordination in 1914 until the Second Vatican Council, Martin Hellriegel led worshiping assemblies, as did other pastors like him, in vigorous, shared, spiritually alive celebrations of the liturgy—all within the severely restricted framework of unreformed Latin rites. In other words, the pioneers,

---

4. Kavanagh, *The Shape of Baptism: The Rite of Christian Initiation* (New York: Pueblo, 1978); Rutherford, *The Death of a Christian: The Rite of Funerals* (New York: Pueblo, 1980); Richstatter, *Liturgical Law: New Style, New Spirit* (Chicago: Franciscan Herald Press, 1977); Seasoltz, *New Liturgy, New Laws* (Collegeville, Minn.: The Liturgical Press, 1980).

both in their parish practice and in the usages they expounded and urged, made the very most of what they had. They took advantage of every opportunity they could find within the static Latin liturgy, under constraints we would find almost incomprehensible today. The lesson to us should be plain.

The fact is that the pioneers were a good deal less reformers than pedagogues and presiders, animators of liturgy, and proclaimers. The Liturgical Conference, for example, kept at arm's length from the Vernacular Society lest the legitimate desires of the latter compromise the primary interests of the Conference in liturgical formation and celebration. Martin Hellriegel himself was indeed a reformer, sometimes tentative, sometimes bold, and a vernacularist, but this was always secondary to the celebration of the liturgy of the time, however rigid or constrained its pattern.

I will indulge in a single anecdote. At the Assisi Congress of 1956, there was a social gathering of the English-speaking participants. Our British brethren — there were, I think, no sisters — were perhaps the forerunners of the membership of the Latin Mass Society. Hellriegel gently made the point of the vernacularists by addressing the gathering in correct Latin; some of the British got the point.

Today, the example of those who made the most of a rigid liturgical pattern and discipline may be helpful. For one thing, I will not tire of saying that we have barely begun to uncover the potential of the present rites, aside from further reform and adaptation, however desirable the latter may be. For another thing, we surely seem to be in a period of constraints if not retrenchment. And such constraints, realistically and perhaps understandably, are greater in parish worship than in house, school, campus, or small-group liturgies.

The recent eucharistic instruction is a small sign of this constraint, not at all threatening in itself, but surely an indication that the openness to liturgical accommodation and acculturation, solemnly determined by the college of bishops in 1963, is closed or in suspense. And I suppose that if a list of aberrations and concerns is needed, we could match each one in the instruction with a more grievous sin of liturgical omission. At the same time, we should be pleased that there are almost no new restraints in it—merely restatements of discipline—and that the document is by no means as incrementally negative as the cautionary instruction of September 1970.

There are indications enough that, prescinding from further development and adaptation, important as they are, we are not yet taking much advantage of what we have in the revised liturgy of the Eucharist and the other sacraments. Articles and letters on liturgical silence and the like during the past year show how highly educated, sophisticated, and insightful persons can be unaware that the reformed Order of Mass deliberately introduced periods of conscious silence into the Eucharist where there had been none before. Defects the reform has, but not that one. For the first time, formal, religious silence—liturgical silence, if you will—has been added to the Roman rite, not the accidental silence of preconciliar days because the priest neglected to speak up or parts of the sung liturgy were curtailed or omitted. Many criticisms of the reform are justified; more are not. Criticisms arise because we have failed to enrich the basic rite as directed or have simply gone through the prescribed motions, words, and gestures, almost as an old-fashioned rubrician would have expected.

In a way, this is the point at which the pioneers put us to shame. With extraordinary constraints, with much less to work with, with fewer options and alternatives in the appointed liturgy, they were genuinely creative. We can be no less, even given the current hesitations and apparent retrenchment, if not regression, in officialdom.

The Order of Mass, whether considered normative or typical or simply basic, illustrates this lesson. Perhaps more than the other sacramental rites, it was designed as the framework on which to build—to enrich, to enliven, to develop. Objectively viewed, it is light years ahead — although very venerable in principle and precedent — of the Order of Mass of 1570 with which our liturgical pioneers had to work, in Latin at that. Much as we might desire and work for the improvement of the present Order of Mass, we can hardly complain until we have really exhausted its possibilities.

My third and final point is brief and rather elusive. I am happy to say that some attitudes are not found in the liturgical pioneers. For example, they seem not to have thought that liturgical change or the liturgy itself would cure the ills of Church and society; this, I may say in criticism, appears to be the trap of false expectations into which newcomers to liturgical involvement fell in the late sixties. The pioneers seem also to have avoided giving offense to established pieties — no iconoclasm, no refusals to bless people or things, no scorn for the ignorant, no fads or few fads. And they appear to have had little fear of excesses of didacticism in liturgy, excesses we have had reason to fear.

Perhaps this final lesson, concerning a didactic liturgy, can be learned from the liturgical pioneers, although it requires more exploration than I can give it. Hellriegel correctly phrased the question: the liturgy is "celebration not demonstration," but he himself employed every kind of imaginative device with didactic and educative force. Today we still have not achieved a happy marriage of liturgy and catechetics or become comfortable with what the Constitution on the Liturgy (33-36) considers the didactic or formative nature of the liturgy.

We have certainly learned that the homily is, like the reading of the word, a proclamation and celebration of God's saving deeds in Jesus and now in us, rather than a sharing of religious information, a mere communication of ideas, a catechetical or exegetical analysis and instruction. There remains a threat, but only a diminished threat, that the seven Sundays of Easter will be devoted to a scholastic analysis of the seven deadly sins or even the seven wonders of the ancient world. And there must be no retreat from what we have learned: the liturgy of praise and confession of God's goodness must not be used, in any of its parts, as a substitute for catechesis.

On the other hand, perhaps we should have the confidence which the liturgical pioneers seemed to have and let the liturgy work its formative and educative way, as the Constitution on the Liturgy proposes. The experience of celebration—whether the songs we sing, the words and music we hear, the prayer to which we conform our own thought—is indeed formative for the whole assembly, including its ministers. The fact that the liturgy does not and should not have a direct didactic or pedagogical purpose does not weaken its impact or its force as a teacher. Especially in the parish context, those who plan, prepare, and preside over liturgies should have a clear awareness of this dimension. It need not hurt the proclamatory and celebratory dimension, which are primary. It should be kept in mind by everyone, as it surely was by the liturgical pioneers. If the external rites should well up from inner piety, those same externals can also shape and form thoughts and emotions, as Hellriegel and the others understood.

In these several reflections, I have purposely omitted the defects of the pioneering liturgical apostolate in this country as well as the contrasts, cultural and otherwise, between then and now. But I should mention the great difference, to our present advantage. These pioneers and those whom they influenced were, until the Second Vatican Council, a small fraction, a misunderstood elite in the Church community. Today the liturgically concerned, whether favorable or not, are very many, surely the majority of those who take part in the holy mysteries.

I hope this has not sounded like an exhortation to do a little more of just what you have been doing these past few days of this Conference. Certainly the lessons I propose from our predecessors and past models are simple enough: to engage in more profound theoretical liturgical study so that our parish celebration may be the more authentic and effective; to employ to the full in parish worship the opportunities of the current liturgy, whatever the chafing constraints; to permit the parish liturgy itself to form the Christian people without its becoming a didactic enterprise.

It has been a pleasure to join you at Notre Dame for your closing Eucharist and to have had a part in the final session of this important annual Conference, now in its ninth year. It has been an honor to share in a deserved tribute to a great and grand pioneer of the American liturgical movement — and to have provided these slight reflections as a substitute for his grateful response to the Michael Mathis Award.